also by Harold Nicolson

KING GEORGE V: HIS LIFE AND REIGN
GOOD BEHAVIOUR: BEING A STUDY
OF CERTAIN TYPES OF CIVILITY
THE EVOLUTION OF DIPLOMATIC METHOD
THE CONGRESS OF VIENNA 1812–1822
LORD CARNOCK
PEACEMAKING 1919
CURZON: THE LAST PHASE 1919–1925
BENJAMIN CONSTANT
BYRON: THE LAST JOURNEY
TENNYSON: ASPECTS OF HIS LIFE, CHARACTER
AND POETRY
HELEN'S TOWER
THE DESIRE TO PLEASE

The
English Sense
of Humour
and other
essays

Harold Nicolson

'What this vision may mean, ye men that are merry,
Discern ye! I dare not discern it myself.'

PIERS THE PLOWMAN

Funk & Wagnalls • *New York*

CONTENTS

AUTHOR'S NOTE

The English Sense of Humour was published in a limited edition by the Dropmore Press in 1946. The consideration of *The Health of Authors* was made to the Royal College of Physicians as the Lloyd Roberts Lecture for 1947. The essay on *Tennyson's Two Brothers* formed the Leslie Stephen Lecture delivered to the University of Cambridge in 1947. The study of *Swinburne and Baudelaire* was the Zaharoff Lecture given at Oxford in 1930. The article on *Alexander the Great* was written for the New York magazine *Life*. The examination of *Nature in Greek Poetry* was the theme of the Presidential address made to the Classical Association in 1951.

My grateful thanks are due to the Institutions, Authorities and publishers above-mentioned for permission to reprint these articles, lectures and addresses.

H. N.

I

THE ENGLISH SENSE
OF HUMOUR

Some explanation is required at the outset regarding the terminology which will be used. The simplest way in which to define the 'sense' of something is to begin by defining what that something is. If I can make it plain what hearing is, or what touch is, then I shall experience no great difficulty in explaining a sense of hearing or a sense of touch. Unfortunately the word 'humour' does not lend itself to any precise definition.

The English words which we apply currently to the many manifestations of the laughable are numerous and vague. We have the comic, the ludicrous, the ridiculous, the quaint, the droll, the jocular, the facetious, the waggish, the bantering, the farcical. We have wit, irony, satire, sarcasm, fancy, mockery, joke, quirk, pun, tomfoolery, clowning, glee, the burlesque, the mock-heroic and what is known as 'innocent mirth'. Each of these words implies a variation of the laughable; some of them are ingredients of a sense of humour; others are not. The word 'humour' is itself employed in many variable ways. Sometimes it is used in the objective sense to describe events or associations which are productive of laughter; sometimes it is used in the subjective sense to describe the appreciation of the laughable. Thus when we say that a situation is 'not entirely devoid of humour' we mean that it contains elements which make us laugh: but when we say that a person is 'entirely devoid of humour' we mean that he is incapable of seeing certain kinds of joke. The indiscriminate manner in which we use the word 'humour' becomes even more apparent when we observe how it changes its meaning according to the epithet which we attach to it. There is, for instance, a recognisable difference between 'grim back and slight lifting of the corners of the mouth, the raising of the upper lip, the formation of wrinkles under the eyes, and an increased brightness of the eyes due to the contraction of the cheek muscles. Secondly, the chuckle, in which these facial movements spread to the larynx. Thirdly, the laugh, whereby the chest muscles become affected, an interruption occurs in the normal rhythm of the respiratory processes, the speech mechanism assumes an aspirate position, and those paroxysmal expirations follow which we call 'laughter'. If the sensation of amusement be very strongly stimulated or much prolonged, then a fourth series of movements results. The muscles affected successively by the smile, the chuckle and the laugh do not afford sufficient relief to the acquired nervous tension; the eyes begin to water and the victim indulges in further spasmodic movements, such as clapping hands or slapping thighs.

It is contended also by those who wish to stress the uniformity of laughter that these physical symptoms are not confined to civilised man. We are assured that all savages, with the possible exception of the laughless Weddas of Ceylon, smile and laugh in the same manner as we do ourselves. The anthropoid apes, as Darwin noticed, will when tickled emit 'a reiterated sound, corresponding to our laughter'. Dogs smile infrequently, but when they do (as at the sudden humiliation of another dog) their facial muscles fall into the same curves as those of the human grin. There is no reason to suppose however that, because only some animals laugh as we do, other animals are never amused. And I doubt whether all savages, when amused, indulge in the same facial contortions, or utter the same sounds, as we do ourselves. I met a Dinka once in Malakal who, being entranced by the spectacle of a white man falling prone upon the sand from the step-ladder of an aeroplane, emitted a low hoot, raised his hands on high so that his bracelets rattled down his arms like rings upon a wooden curtain rod, and then unsmilingly resumed his heron-like pose. He may, it is true, have been assailed by sudden reverence; but he was assuredly amused; and he did not express his amusement by the guffaw of civilised man. I consider it unproven, therefore, that all who laugh do so in the same way.

Before I leave the physiology of laughter there is a further point which I wish to consider. Many people have asked themselves why sensations of amusement should result in contractions, first of the facial muscles and thereafter of the larynx and the chest muscles. Herbert Spencer suggested that the overflow of nerve force undirected by any motive will necessarily take the most habitual route: that speech is the most habitual route: and that it is for this reason that certain muscles situated around the mouth are the first to be affected.

Dr. Sully advances a different, and for my purposes a more significant, theory. He observed that in the human infant the smile precedes the laugh by some two or three months. The first smile of the infant is, in his opinion, caused by satisfied appetite; only at a later stage is a smile evoked by other sensations of pleasure, such as recognition. It is thus natural that the smile, originating as it does from satisfaction at being fed, should be expressed by movements of the lips. This observation leads Dr. Sully to the contention

that the smile occurs at the level of sensation, whereas
the laugh occurs at the level of perception; or in other
words that the smile is the expression of feeling,
whereas the laugh is the expression of thought. Now
it will be agreed that the sense of humour expresses
itself physiologically not always by laughter, seldom
by uproarious laughter, but more usually by the
chuckle or the smile. I admit of course that with cul-
tivated adults the smile is for other reasons often
preferred to the noises of laughter, but the point of
Dr. Sully's observation remains unaffected by this circumstance. Thus the physiology, and observed evolution, of laughter suggest at the outset that the level
of consciousness at which the sense of humour operates
is somewhere between sensation and perception, somewhere between feeling and thought; and that it par-
takes of both.

It is permissible, before we go any further, to
exclude from our considerations all forms of laughter
which have nothing to do with sensations of amusement, or even with sensations of pleasure. It may well
be that lunatics, as Heymans remarked, laugh from
'satisfied vanity'; yet there is no pleasure, and still less
amusement, in hysterical laughter, which is no more
than the discharge of abnormal nervous tension. It
may be argued also that there exists no specific sensation of amusement in the perfunctory smile of
greeting, the smile of polite attention, the smile of
social embarrassment, the smile of domestic affection,
or the smile of nervous hesitation. We sometimes
laugh when released suddenly from physical or mental
strain; when immersed in icy water; when we inhale
nitrous oxide or nitrite of amyl. Such manifestations

are little more than physiological reactions and, as Theodor Lipps observed, 'give us no information of value regarding the nature of the laughable'. They will be excluded from this discussion under the heading of 'abnormal laughter'.

3

It seems strange to me that many clever and cautious men have been so misled by the circumstance that sensations of amusement often express themselves in similar muscular contractions as to imagine that something which produces a common effect must derive from a common cause. The several theories which have been evolved to explain the nature of the laughable throw a penetrating light upon one or other of the many causes of laughter; but when an attempt is made to ascribe to a single cause all the many variations of the ludicrous it is found that much of what is laughable is excluded from the particular synthesis and much is included which is not laughable in the least.

The connection between the smile, the chuckle and the laugh on the one hand, and on the other the sensation of amusement, seems to me to be no more constant or immediate than the connection between tears and sorrow. Unhappiness also produces a whole series of physical symptoms; but the fact that most people cry in the same sort of manner has not tempted any serious philosopher to lay down a single formula for misery. I thus agree with Jean Paul Richter that 'the laughable has from the beginning refused to enter into the definitions of philosophers, except unwillingly'. What surprises me is that this unwillingness should not have been more marked.

Although, therefore, I believe that sensations of amusement are variable and complex rather than constant and simple, I shall find it useful, if I wish to isolate the English sense of humour, briefly to examine some of the main theories which have been advanced as explanations of the laughable. There are four main formulas which the philosophers and the psychologists have devised. In suggesting that all laughter can be explained by their own particular theory these wise men are suggesting something absurd. But their formulas do certainly furnish descriptions of some of the main causes of laughter and as such they must assuredly be examined. The four theories which I have in mind are the following: (1) the theory of self-esteem; (2) the theory of descending incongruity; (3) the theory of release from constraint; and (4) the theory of automatism as opposed to free activity.

(1) La Rochefoucauld contended that 'in the misfortunes of our friends there is always something that pleases us'. This was no new idea. Aristotle used the word 'ἐπιχαιρεκακία, or as the Germans would say *Schadenfreude*, to describe the amusement which is aroused in human beings by the 'dangerless' misfortunes or infirmities of their fellow mortals. Cicero repeated this conception when he asserted that laughter 'is never far removed from derision'; and Professor Alexander Bain, in more modern terms, defines 'the occasion of the ludicrous' as 'the degradation of some person or interest possessing dignity in circumstances that excite no other strong emotion'.

It was Thomas Hobbes who first ascribed to heightened self-esteem the pleasure which some that the reverse is true. I should not say however that Hobbes's 'sudden glory' is wholly absent from the several ingredients of which the English sense of humour is composed. Since although it does not operate in its positive form, that is in the form of derision, it does arise in a negative form, that is, in the form of extreme sensitiveness to the derision of others. Such 'sudden glory' as we may derive from the superiority-inferiority relation is not, in so far as the sense of humour is concerned, caused by the realisation of superiority in ourselves or of inferiority in others; it is caused by the sudden relief which we experience when, in circumstances of personal humil-iation or diffidence, we successfully apply the pro-tective mechanism of the sense of humour to our own inferiority, or, as Hobbes remarked, to 'ourselves formerly'. Much will be said hereafter regarding this protective function of the sense of humour.

(2) It was Herbert Spencer who invented the phrase 'descending incongruity'. He contended that the in-congruous only became laughable 'when consciousness is unawares transferred from great things to small—only when there is what we may call a "descending incongruity"'. He illustrated his point by suggesting that an 'ascending incongruity' (when the expectedly small becomes the unexpectedly great) does not pro-duce amusement but wonder; and that the physical symptoms of wonder are the very opposite of those caused by amusement; namely the relaxation of the facial muscles (as in the dropping of the jaw) and not their contraction. This view is supported by other writers. Kant, in an incidental remark, defined laughter as 'an affection arising from the sudden transformation

of a strained expectation into nothing'. 'Laughter', writes Theodor Lipps, 'arises when something significant or impressive suddenly loses its significance or impressiveness.' How far does this explanation or formula apply to the English sense of humour?

Let me examine for a moment one of the classic illustrations of a descending incongruity. On some festive occasion I prepare to release fireworks. I establish a rocket in a field at a safe distance from the house and when darkness comes I summon the children and the household to witness the event. If I am a fussy or self-important man, I spend much time in marshalling my audience in such a manner as will remove them from the area of possible danger. But when I come to light my rocket the only result is a faint splutter; nothing happens; and general laughter follows. The cause of this laughter is clearly the sudden denial of expectation (much enhanced by my elaborate preparations), and the transformation of something into nothing. But if the rocket had in fact soared into the night sky, spreading gold and emeralds and rubies against the dark, then wonder, and a general intake of breath, would have resulted: not guffaws.

Supposing, however, that among the twelve people of all ages and every grade of sensibility who witnessed the failure of my demonstration there was one man who refrained from joining in the general laughter. This solitary agelast would be viewed by the other eleven with feelings of hostility. They might, in their different ways, suppose him to be aloof, arrogant, morose, conceited, inhuman, affected, ill-tempered, absent-minded, in love, or very ill. The accusation that he was 'deficient in a sense of humour' would not be the accusation which would occur most naturally to their minds. If we submit to this test other descending incongruities we shall find that the same principle applies. Thus we laugh at a clergyman sneezing in the middle of his sermon, at an elderly man wearing a child's hat, at a person lifting an object which appears to be heavy and turns out to be light, at a mouse darting across the floor of the House of Commons: but if we failed to laugh at such events we should not naturally or rightly be accused of lacking a sense of humour; we should be accused of possessing no sense of the comic or no sense of fun.

Is there anything to be learnt from these illustrations? I think there is. They imply that the sense of humour, as distinct from the sense of the comic, is affected, not by a sudden manifestation of the incongruous, but by a gradual realisation of the incongruous. This is a significant difference. It suggests that the sense of humour, unlike the appreciation of wit, does not require the stimulus of condensation and surprise. It suggests also that the sense of humour entails processes which are slower than those of the physical or immediate reaction; that it is an attitude of mind rather than an activity of mind; that it is a contemplative subconscious habit rather than an intuitive flash; and it suggests that when Herbert Spencer used the phrase 'when consciousness is unawares transferred from great things to small' he was attributing importance to the word 'unawares'.

(3) The third general formula or explanation is that laughter is no more than the sudden incoming of gladness produced by release from constraint. In its simplest forms, this type of laughter is produced

by physical release, as when little boys laugh loudly when dismissed from school. In its more complex form, it is provoked by what Professor John Dewey calls 'a termination of effort' and is in this sense akin to a sigh of relief. It can arise from the sudden adjustment of reason to unreason, or in other words from enlightenment after confusion. It can be provoked also, as Kräpelin has observed, by the liberation of natural impulses from the discipline of the social pattern. Freud has argued that this release is occasioned (especially when amusement is derived from obscene jokes) by the pleasurable discharge of accumulated inhibitions.

The type of laughter produced by release from constraint, or by a sudden rush of irreverence, is undoubtedly an important component of the sense of humour. But here again the sense of humour is not concerned with every release from constraint, but only with certain forms of release. The little boys, for instance, who dash laughing across the playground are not indulging in a sense of humour; they are indulging in high spirits. Being undemonstrative, the sense of humour does not *celebrate* release, it *enjoys* freedom; being passive, it does not assail constraint, it seeks to pretend that constraint is not irksome.

(4) In his delightful book, *Le Rire*, Henri Bergson has advanced many incidental ideas, and one central theory, which provide much fresh and valuable information regarding the nature of some forms of laughter. In his view society demands two qualities from its members, namely (*a*) awareness, and (*b*) adaptability. When a person rejects these demands by becoming either absent-minded or rigid, then society is rendered

uneasy and applies to the recalcitrant the sanction of ridicule. The central, as the most original, theory which Bergson propounds is that people laugh when confronted 'by a certain mechanical rigidity (*raideur de mécanique*) when they expect the suppleness and flexibility of the human being'. Any substitution of the mechanical for the human is intrinsically comic. Thus a repeated gesture amuses us in an orator, not necessarily because it is ludicrous in itself, but because by its repetition it suggests the functioning of the machine.

Mimicry makes us laugh in that it brings out the mechanical, or repetitive, in a given personality. We laugh when the form of something imposes itself upon the content, as when we observe old-fashioned hats, professionalism or red-tape. If human beings were constantly on the alert, these relapses into the mechanical would not occur; they occur in moments of inattention or absent-mindedness. And thus for Bergson the main cause of laughter is the treatment of life 'as if it were a machine, which could repeat, which could be reversed, and which has interchangeable parts'.

It will be agreed that many sensations of amusement are in fact aroused by Bergson's formula of 'automatism as opposed to free activity'. Some of the situations in which human beings behave like animals or things are undoubtedly humorous situations; but not all such situations. I was recently on the top of a bus in Regent Street when an elderly lady on the pavement stumbled over a protruding step and fell to the ground. There were two little boys on the top of the bus who, observing this incident, burst into peals of delighted laughter; the adult passengers were moved, not by ridicule, but by compassion. The lady in falling had certainly been guilty of inadaptability and inadvertence; she had behaved as an inanimate object; but we did not laugh, and our sudden seriousness could not rightly have been ascribed to a deficient sense of humour. This example suggests that although appreciation of the contrast between flexibility and rigidity is a component of the sense of humour, the resultant laughter or seriousness depends, not so much upon the nature of the event, as upon the level at which the event impinges on the consciousness.

To define the level of consciousness at which the English sense of humour operates will not be an easy or a popular task. Before I approach this task I must first consider how the sense of humour differs from the appreciation of wit, irony and satire, and what are the several meanings which the word 'humour' has assumed at different periods and in different countries.

Meanwhile it will be useful, before concluding this section, to recapitulate the nine suggestions which have so far been advanced: (1) That laughter is not uniform but multiform. We do not always laugh when amused, and we are not always amused when we laugh. (2) The word 'humour' is employed to mean several different things. (3) The smile and the chuckle are not incomplete laughs but occur at different levels of consciousness. (4) Since the sense of humour expresses itself most frequently, not by the laugh, but by the smile and the chuckle, it also must operate at a special level of consciousness. (5) The sense of humour is not concerned with abnormal laughter. (6) It is not derisive, but is employed as a protective mechanism against the derision of others. (7) It is not

even opposed to, conceptual logic. Thus whereas wit
is the product of imagination and seeks by mental
energy and speed to discover similarities in dissimilar
things, humour is the play of fancy and is content with
the comparatively effortless recognition of dissimilarity
in similar things.

It is this presence or absence of an object and an
intention which also distinguishes humour from satire
and irony. Humour essentially is a receiving station,
not a transmitter; it observes human frailty indulgently
and without bothering to correct it; irony and satire
have a nobler and more didactic purpose. Whereas
irony, being critical and pessimistic, demonstrates the
difference between the real and the ideal, humour,
being uncritical and optimistic, either ignores the
difference, or pretends that it is not, after all, so very
important. One of the main distinctions, for instance,
between American and English humour is that,
whereas the former is ironical in tendency and therefore seeks to make the fantastic seem humiliatingly
real, the latter finds it more comfortable to make the
real appear charmingly fantastic.

Englishmen regard their sense of humour as a cosy,
comfortable, contemplative, lazy and good-humoured
sort of thing. How comes it therefore that to foreigners
the English sense of humour appears atrabilious and
dour? This error, if it be an error, may in part be
due to the origins of the word 'humour' and to the
many misconceptions to which these origins have
given rise.

The Oxford English Dictionary, as always, provides
valuable information. The word 'humour' is derived
from the Latin *humor*, signifying moisture. In medieval

physiology the word was used to denote the fluids or 'cardinal humours' (blood, phlegm, choler, melancholy) according to the relative proportions of which a person's bodily constitution and emotional disposition were supposed to be determined. The medical origins of the word are interesting, partly because humour is thereby associated, as Baldensperger points out, with individual temperament; and partly because its inclusion among the cardinal fluids has induced many foreigners to accept false attributions. Thus in France the word 'humour', as first used by Addison, was translated by *humeur*, thereby becoming associated with such misfortunes as black choler and spleen. In Germany, until Lessing pointed out the error, it was translated as *Laune*, which suggested a mood, a fantasy or a whim. Even when the French ceased talking about *humeur* and began to speak of *l'humour anglais*, the old atrabilious associations remained. Thus Taine, whose knowledge of England and English literature was wide, described our humour as 'the irruption of violent joviality, buried under a heap of melancholy, to which are added flashes of unexpected imagination'. In his *Notes on England* which were written between 1861 and 1871, occurs the following startling passage:

'It matters not [to the English] if French wit be lacking. They possess a form of it for their own use, which, although far from agreeable, is certainly original, powerful, poignant and slightly bitter to the taste, as are their national beverages. They call it 'humour'. Generally it is the pleasantry of a man who, while joking maintains his gravity. Sometimes it leads to buffoonery, sometimes to studied sarcasm. It affects the nerves powerfully; it be-

comes lastingly imprinted on the memory. It is the product either of imaginative drollery or of concentrated
indignation. It delights in startling contrasts and in unexpected disguises; it clothes reason in the garments of
madness and madness in the garments of reason. The man
who jests in England is seldom kindly and never happy.
He feels, and forcibly censures, the inequalities of life:
this yields him no amusement, since he suffers inwardly
and is irritated.'

In Volume V of Taine's *History of English Literature*,
in the section devoted to Thomas Carlyle, there occurs
the following passage which is equally curious and
illuminating:

'This turn of mind produces "humour"—a word which
cannot be translated into French, since we do not possess
the quality. "Humour" is that species of talent which may
suffice to amuse the Teutonic races, the men of the North;
it suits their intelligence, even as beer and brandy suit
their palates. For people of another race it is disagreeable;
our nerves find it too sharp and bitter.'

Bergson also to some extent shares the French misconception of the nature of English humour:

'Humour [he writes] is the opposite of irony. Each of
them is a form of satire, but irony is by its nature ora-
torical, whereas humour has a scientific aspect. One
stresses irony by allowing oneself to be raised higher
and higher by the thought of the good that ought to
be; it is for this reason that irony can heat itself internally
so as to become in some way eloquence under pressure.
One accentuates humour on the contrary by descending
deeper and deeper into the evil that exists, in order to
note its peculiarities with the coldest indifference. Many
authors, and Jean Paul among them, have noted that
humour is partial to concrete terms, to technical details,

to precise facts. If our analysis be correct, this is no adventitious element in humour, but its very essence. The humorist is a moralist who disguises himself as a scientist, something like an anatomist who dissects bodies in order only to create disgust. Thus humour, in the restricted sense in which we are using the word, is really the transposition of morals into science.'

To those who regard the English sense of humour as an amiable and contented quality, these judgements may appear harsh and incorrect. Yet it is always an error to dismiss as ignorant or fantastic the comments of intelligent foreigners, especially of foreigners who have devoted many years of life to the study of our thought and manners. Taine is certainly correct in stating that there exists in the English sense of humour a special combination of mockery and gravity; that it represents a nervous rather than an intellectual reaction; that it assumes unexpected disguises; that it is indigenous and possesses a strong imaginative quality; and that it sometimes degenerates into buffoonery and childishness.

Few people would deny that the love of nonsense which is so significant a component of the English sense of humour amounts to 'clothing reason in the garments of madness and madness in the garments of reason'. But most people would maintain that Taine and Bergson are labouring under a misconception when they assert that the English sense of humour possesses a 'scientific' or realistic element; that it is melancholy in tone and bitter to the taste; that it is seldom kindly and never happy; or that it is based upon a concentrated indignation with the inequalities of existence.

Such people may seek to explain the disturbing discrepancy between the French and the British conception of English humour by contending that Taine was writing as a student of our literature, and that his remarks apply not to our modern and so lambent sense of humour, but to that which existed in the seventeenth and eighteenth centuries. They will argue that Taine was not thinking of sweet and simple humorists, such as our contemporaries J. M. Barrie and A. A. Milne, but of harsh humorists such as Swift and the darker Dickens. I readily admit that Taine's definitions are not at all applicable to the fattened sense of humour which is so amply provided for in the pages of *Punch*. But they do furnish a correct description of the leaner type of humour which is that of the English working classes, and which we sometimes call 'cockney' humour and sometimes 'sardonic' humour. This type of humour is assuredly not complacent, escapist or bland; it is realistic, sceptical, cynical, indignant, frequently obscene, sometimes scatological, and in tone and intent both bitter and harsh.

Am I suggesting that there are two English senses of humour, the one sardonic and possessed by the proletariat, the other gentle and indulged in only by the *bourgeoisie*? I am making no such distinctions. The encouraging thing about the English sense of humour is that it is a national quality possessed by all classes alike. The poor are amused by the same forms of the laughable as are the rich, the only difference being the degrees of subtlety apprehended by the educated or the uneducated. The propertied classes, on the other hand, have a very lively appreciation of cockney humour and regard it with affection. I am contending only that the sardonic elements, which Taine rightly included in his definitions, and which give a tart taste to so much of English proletarian humour, are not to be confused with 'humour' in the sense which I am using that word, but should more correctly be described as 'irony'. For if I am correct in contending that one of the main features of 'humour' is that it is entirely purposeless, then with the intrusion of irony it ceases to be 'humour' and becomes something else.

Although it is not my intention (at least in this essay) to examine the nature of English proletarian humour—or as I should prefer to say of 'English proletarian irony'—or to draw attention to its remarkable ingenuity, richness and strength, yet there is one special element in proletarian irony which has overflowed, so to speak, into the English sense of humour and which constitutes one of its most unexpected characteristics. I refer to what we sometimes call 'grim humour' and what the Germans call *Galgenhumor*—an expression which means something more than our own expression 'gallows humour'. By 'grim humour' I mean the humorous treatment of the tragic or the horrible.

This species of joke is peculiarly English, although incidentally it represents one of the many elements which English and Scottish humour have in common. Thus of the thirty-six 'notions' in which Sam Weller indulges in the *Pickwick Papers* as many as twenty-four are concerned with truly horrible events. Without a moment's remorse the younger Weller will illustrate the relation between ends and means by an analogy such as 'As the father said ven he cut his little boy's head off to cure him of squinting.' This type of 'notion' has in recent years assumed a slightly

American mode, but its essence remains the same. I am indebted to a friend for the following authentic transcription of a 'notion' uttered in a B.A.O.R. canteen: 'The wife's uncle was blown clean through the wardrobe and we never found so much as a button. I had to laugh.' It was doubtless this form of proletarian gibe which grated so unpleasantly upon the nerves of Taine.

If therefore I am correct in asserting that 'sardonic' humour is a different thing from 'gentle' humour, and that, being ironical in its nature and purpose, it has little to do with that species of humour which we identify with the English sense of humour, I must now enquire what is the element, the presence or absence of which differentiates the gentle from the sardonic. That element is sympathy.

There are two aspects of 'gentle' humour upon which most investigators are agreed. First, that it is a matter of temperament, or in other words that it is concerned less with thought than with a general attitude towards life. Secondly, that it is a private rather than a public indulgence; that it is individual rather than choral. 'Unlike wit,' writes Coleridge, 'humour does not consist wholly in the understanding or the senses. There must exist some peculiarity of the individual temperament as a cause of the disproportion. It must imply a growth from within.' 'The essence of humour', writes Lipps more lucidly, 'is not of course some humorous action but a way of feeling and thinking.' To Dr. Sully humour is not the 'swift reflex gaiety' of a child or the untutored savage; it has nothing to do with choral merriment; it is the private laughter of the developed individual.

We can readily agree with the last assertion since we are all conscious that our sense of humour is a more intimate, a more confidential, source of amused sensation than our other appreciations of the ludicrous; it occupies a private place in the heart. And whereas our appreciations of wit, satire and irony are always mental appreciations, our sense of humour is a diffused feeling in which sensation and perception are combined. It is the 'sympathetic quality' of the sense of humour which, while it differentiates it from wit, irony and satire, associates it with pathos and often with sentimentality.

5

I now propose to take my argument a stage further and to examine at what level of consciousness the English sense of humour operates.

It is tempting for this purpose to adopt the fiction that all laughter can be divided into the two categories of 'spontaneous' and 'reflective', and to proceed as if this fiction were valid.

By Spontaneous Laughter I mean the laughter which arises from instinctive, primal, or elementary sensations of amusement. In such laughter there is comparatively little reflective or mental quality; there is no clear perception of relations; although arising from a specific cause, it possesses no specific object, motive or purpose; it represents an immediate, almost physical, response to an event; as such it is akin to a physiological reaction.

The sensations of amusement which result in spontaneous laughter are aroused by many different causes. Of these various causes, I give the following ten examples: (1) High spirits, whether produced by a general sense of well-being, or by sudden release from fear, difficulty, confusion or constraint. (2) All forms of play, including word play, parody, puns and nonsense. (3) Amicable teasing and even practical jokes so long as the sensations of amusement are not checked by other sensations, such as sympathy, fear, pity or disgust. (4) Physical incongruities, deformities, and the grotesque. (5) The unfamiliar, the new, the superior, the sophisticated, the old-fashioned. (6) Some obvious breach of uniformity, such as soldiers marching out of step, or social solecisms. (7) Dangerless misfortunes in others, such as small accidents, seasickness or toothache. (8) Obscenity and sex jokes. (9) The more obvious manifestations of incongruity or inconsequence, as when the disparity between intention and performance becomes blatantly apparent. (10) Clowning, buffoonery and horse-play.

Reflective Laughter, on the other hand, entails a greater degree of mental activity. It arises less from sensation than from perception; it requires a more alert realisation of values and a more sensitive awareness of relations; and above all it is not, as is Spontaneous Laughter, entirely purposeless, but carries with it some implied criticism, either of life in general, or of the faults, follies or pretensions of an individual.

I choose the following seven examples of reflective laughter: (1) Wit. (2) Satire. (3) Irony and Sarcasm. (4) Derision. (5) The unmasking of the pretentious, such as false dignity, pomposity, or snobbishness. (6) The exposure of moral deformities, such as rigidity, false values, self-satisfied ignorance, or slow understanding. (7) The subtler forms of incongruity, contrariety and inconsequence, namely those which require for their perception a delicately balanced sense of proportion.

The value of this fiction is that it indicates that the English sense of humour lies somewhere in between what I have called 'spontaneous laughter' and what I have called 'reflective laughter', partaking of each and yet being slightly closer to the former than to the latter. Thus of the ten examples I have given under Spontaneous Laughter, seven are clearly concerned with the sense of humour whereas three are not. Conversely, of the seven examples I have given of Reflective Laughter, four must be excluded from a sense of humour and three included. It would be agreed, that is, that high spirits, teasing, and the pleasure derived from the misfortunes of others have little to do with the sense of humour; whereas all forms of play, the grotesque, the unfamiliar, all breaches of uniformity, obscenity, blatant incongruity and clowning affect the very sensations of amusement of which the sense of humour is composed. It will be agreed, on the other hand, that, whereas wit, irony, satire and derision are not true components of a sense of humour, the instinctive recognition of the pretentious, of moral and intellectual deformities, and of the subtler forms of incongruity are all matters with which the sense of humour is closely and continuously concerned.

Let me adopt another fiction. Supposing it were possible to define the grades of the ludicrous as accurately as we can define the temperature; and that we could produce a thermometer of the laughable on which the several degrees could be marked on a scale rising from 0 to 100. Supposing that degrees 0–40 represented the lower levels, starting from the purely physiological reaction and reaching at about 25 degrees the elementary laughter of children and very simple people. Supposing that degrees 70–100 represented the highest levels of sophisticated laughter, namely those occasions of laughter which require for their perception a high order of mental energy. Then under my contention the English sense of humour would fall somewhere in the area between 20 and 55.

I fear that in giving to the English sense of humour so comparatively humble a position in the class, I shall be causing pain to those who regard their own sense of humour, not merely as a private paraclete, but as the sponsor and announcer of their own sensibility and charm. I hope, before I have finished, to bring some comfort to such tender souls.

The two fictions which I have adopted furnish some indications of the level of consciousness at which the sense of humour most frequently operates. Useful information on the subject can also be obtained by considering the evolution of human laughter.

Freud, in his *Wit and Its Relation to the Unconscious*, makes the suggestion that laughter passes through three evolutionary stages. First comes the play of childhood, including the rudimentary forms of word-play by which pleasure is derived from the association of sound rather than of sense. Secondly comes the joke, by which the adult seeks to reproduce the delights of child-play without exposing himself to the reproof of childishness. And thirdly comes wit, which enables the intelligent person to render his jokes sophisticated and as such flattering to the mind.

The sequence—(1) play; (2) jokes; (3) wit—is a suggestive sequence.

The problem has been examined in detail by Dr. Sully in his *Essay on Laughter*. He observed that as the child begins to grasp the ordinary relations between things, his sense of the ludicrous becomes more differentiated. A number of laughters, variously tuned, begin to appear: the child becomes aware of the 'funny'; and with this comes a growing perception of deviation from expected behaviour, namely the inconsequent and the incongruous.

The laughter of savages, on the other hand, does not, if we are to trust the observers, pass through any such process of evolution; it is static and simple. 'It is not child-like,' writes Miss Kingsley of the humour of the West African, 'it is more feminine in quality.' By 'feminine' Miss Kingsley meant, I presume, protective rather than aggressive. All observers agree that savages do not laugh at themselves or at the members of their own tribe. They laugh at other tribes, they laugh at foreigners, they laugh at differences in custom, and they laugh at the new. The Hudson Bay Indians are reported to have roared with laughter at a ship's compass, which they took to be a toy and as such a stimulus to their play-appetite. The natives of Tierra del Fuego were immensely amused when they observed a white man washing his face. All savages find the mispronunciation or misuse of their own language by foreigners irresistibly amusing.

Dr. Sully calls savage-laughter and child-laughter 'primal laughter', and he contends that primal laughter develops into civilised laughter owing to increasing awareness in the individual of his relation to the community. He underlines the importance of the social, or choral, element in laughter, stressing its infectiousness, its employment as a tribal corrective, and its prophylactic value as protecting the community from external contamination. He implies that when individual laughter becomes choral it tends to revert to primal laughter and he confesses that he has found it difficult to recognise in an English music-hall audience 'any distinct traces of a deposit from the advance of the culture stream'.

Dr. Sully therefore would contend that when the sense of humour ceases to be a private enjoyment and becomes public or choral it reverts to 'primal' laughter and adopts the forms of child-laughter and savage-laughter. If this be true (and I believe it to be true) then the evolution of laughter also suggests that, upon my imaginary thermometer, the English sense of humour should be placed in an area ranging from the lower-middle to the middle degrees. It occurs, in other words, at a level of consciousness situated between the upper levels of sensation and the lower levels of perception; and combining both.

6

Having suggested that the English sense of humour operates at a level of consciousness situated between sensation and perception, and therefore partaking of both; having stated that it is concerned, not with every type of humour, but only with those types which are easily apprehended at its own special level; I must now direct my inquiry to the elements of which it is composed.

The first point to examine is whether there does in fact exist such a thing as the English sense of humour; whether, that is, the English temperament is attuned to certain aspects of the laughable in a manner, or to a degree, different from those degrees and manners in which the temperaments of the Scots, the Welsh, the Irish, the Americans, the Germans, or the French are attuned.

It has frequently been asserted that humour, and therefore a sense of humour, is a quality confined to the Nordic races. 'The sunset sky and the damp soil of the North', writes Nencioni in his *L'umorismo et gli umoristi*, 'would seem to be best adapted to the growth of the delicate and strange plant of humour.' Dr. Sully goes so far as to contend that the sense of humour is found only in races of Teutonic stock. It will be admitted that the English sense of humour is far more akin to the German type than to the American or Latin types. The verses of Wilhelm Busch and Morgenstern, the endless variations of the Frau Wirtin saga, appeal more directly to the English sense of humour than they do to that of the French or the Italians. Nor can it be doubted that extreme temperamental lucidity, or the habit of precise and rapid thought, create a climate less favourable to the growth of a sense of humour than the misty imprecisions of the Teutonic lands.

It is possible to contend, moreover, that the English possess certain recognisable qualities and defects of temperament which bear a special relation to their sense of humour. I am not suggesting that other nations do not also possess these qualities and defects: I am suggesting only that they are met with more constantly in England than in other lands. What are these special qualities and defects? I should summarise them as follows:

i. Good-humour. Tolerance. Kindliness. Ready sympathy. Compassion.

ii. An affection for nature, animals and children which sometimes degenerates into sentimentality.

iii. A fund of common sense, which is at once sensible and common to all sections of the community.

iv. A wide and generous gift of fancy.

v. A respect for individual character rather than for individual intelligence. An instinctive sense of human values which reacts unfavourably against any deformation of those values.

vi. A dislike of extremes, over-emphasis, and all forms of boastfulness. A preference for compromise and under-statement.

vii. A love of games and play which often assumes childish forms.

viii. Self-consciousness, diffidence and shyness. A dislike of appearing conspicuous or inviting ridicule.

ix. Laziness, especially mental laziness.

x. Optimism, reflecting itself in a desire for mental and emotional ease.

When we come to examine the components of the English sense of humour we shall find that the pattern they form corresponds very exactly to the pattern formed by these ten qualities and defects. We shall find that the English sense of humour is kindly, sentimental, reasonable, and fanciful; we shall find that it is sensitive to any distortion of individual values, such as affectation, insincerity, vanity, rigidity and all forms of pretension; we shall find that it functions most frequently as the middle path; we shall find that its playfulness, and especially its word-playfulness, possess a childish rather than an adult tone; and we shall find that it functions most frequently as a defence mechanism, protecting the Englishman against the ridicule of others, against the expenditure of excessive mental or psychic energy, against his own diffidence, and against the intrusion of disturbing thoughts and feelings.

If we agree (*a*) that the qualities and defects, which I have enumerated are specifically English qualities and defects and (*b*) that the components of the English sense of humour, which I shall shortly enumerate, correspond closely to these qualities and defects, then we shall be satisfied that the expression 'the English sense of humour' is an expression which does, in fact, possess a definite meaning.

Before I leave this question of the 'Englishness' of a sense of humour there is one further point which must be considered. Is the sense of humour a permanent, or merely a periodic, feature in the English temperament?

It is true that elements which can be distinctly recognised as elements of the sense of humour can be traced right back through Dr. Johnson and Shakespeare to Chaucer and even to Piers Plowman. Yet all the evidence indicates that the sense of humour as a separate area in the English temperament was not *generally recognised* until the last half of the nineteenth century. In all the rich and varied literature of English

invective the first public figure to be accused of possessing no sense of humour was Mr. Gladstone; nobody accused Charles I, or Archbishop Laud, or
Milton, or even Shelley of being deficient in this
attribute; it never occurred to anybody that of the
many and varied privations from which Robinson
Crusoe suffered his lack of any sense of humour was
the most irremediable.

It would seem indeed that a sense of humour can
only flourish nationally when there exists a similarity
of what Santayana calls 'the inner atmosphere and
weather' coincident with widespread individual initi-
ative. It appears to require for its development, on
the one hand a common and assured pattern of convention, and on the other a strong individual desire
to react against that convention. A sense of humour
cannot prosper either in a totalitarian and classless
society or in a society in process of revolution. A
special, fortuitous, and therefore transitory, balance
between acceptance and revolt, between conformity
and noncomformity, between the conventional and
the eccentric, is needed before a sense of humour can
pervade a whole society. Once that balance has been
disturbed, the sense of humour tends either to evap-
orate or to become sectional.

What, therefore, are the specific components of the
English sense of humour? I use the word 'specific' to
indicate that I shall be concerned, not with those
accustomed occasions of the ludicrous which we have
already considered and which arouse sensations of
amusement wherever they occur, but with those occasions which seem laughable to Englishmen and do
not always seem laughable to men of other races. The

English are just as much amused as are other people by the denial of expectation, by descending incongruities, by release from constraint, by automatism as opposed to free activity, or by the unmasking of the false or the pretentious. What is more interesting is that the English sense of humour often assumes special forms and patterns which are different from those assumed by the sensations of amusement experienced by other peoples. What are those special forms and patterns? I shall begin by summarising the specific components of the English sense of humour schematically:

    i.   Kindliness.
    ii.   Sentimentality and pathos.
    iii.   A common basis of sense and tradition.
    iv.   Fancy.
    v.   A special sensitiveness to the distortion of human values.
    vi.   A love of compromise and conciliation.
    vii.   Childishness:
        (*a*) Reversions to childhood.
        (*b*) Child-jokes and the naïve-comic.
        (*c*) Play and word-play.
    viii.   Self-protection:
        (*a*) Against the unfamiliar.
        (*b*) Against danger.
        (*c*) Against the horrible or the tragic.
        (*d*) Against the ridicule of others.
        (*e*) Against intellectual or social superiority.
    ix.   Economy of mental effort:
        (*a*) Love of the familiar. Recognition, repetition, the topical.

(*b*) Laughing at erudition and scholarship.
(*c*) Nonsense.
x. The desire for mental and spiritual ease. The desire for pleasantness.

It will be agreed that of these ten specific components the first six require no detailed examination. It will readily be admitted that the English sense of humour possesses a very large admixture of kindliness, sentiment, reasonableness, and fancy. It will also be admitted that the English are specially sensitive to those distortions of human values which are caused by individual pretensions such as vanity, self-importance, pomposity, rigidity and so on. It will be agreed also that the English sense of humour is conciliatory by nature, that it does not see things in black and white or in terms of conquest or defeat, but that it tends to prefer the middle path and to be suspicious and indeed sceptical of all extremes of brilliance, logic or dogma. More extended analysis is required of the components of childishness, self-protection, economy of mental effort, and the desire for spiritual ease. I shall begin with childishness.

I trust that in considering the childish or primal elements in English laughter I shall not be accused of adopting an unfriendly attitude. I take a normal view of the functions and benefits of laughter and I do not share Lord Chesterfield's distaste. 'Frequent laughter', he wrote, 'is the characteristic of folly and ill manners; it is the manner in which the mob express their silly joy in silly things.' To him laughter was 'a low and unbecoming thing'. 'I am sure', he confessed, 'that since I have had the full use of my reason, nobody has ever heard me laugh.' So far from sharing this adverse opinion, I regard the English sense of humour as a charming attribute and one which serves as a valuable lubricant in the machine of society. I am not therefore seeking to dispraise the English sense of humour; I am seeking only to examine its composition.

That the sense of humour contains a considerable element of the childish or the infantile could scarcely be denied. When assailed by sudden moments of gaiety or well-being we often experience an unconscious reversion to the purposeless laughter of childhood; at times even we derive pleasure by plunging almost deliberately through the crust of adult habituation into the half-remembered freedom of infantile laughter. I have often observed two elderly gentlemen, who have known each other intimately in boyhood, adopt when they meet together a tone of jocularity which is not their usual adult tone but a reversion to their boyhood tone. Such reversions to pre-adult laughter are most infectious, as when a music-hall audience will laugh chorally at jokes or situations which in the individual would not provoke a smile. These are quite normal reversions to the laughter of childhood.

There are occasions, however, when our attempts to recapture lost infantile laughter assume more intricate forms. Freud contends that these occasions are provoked, not by remembered pleasure, but by a sudden comparison between the adult and the childhood condition. At times, for instance, we are amused when adults conduct themselves as children, as when we laugh at clowns and comedians or are entranced by the naïve. At other times we deliberately place ourselves upon the childhood level, and experience amusement from events or situations which arouse childish, but not adult, laughter. And at other times we derive private pleasure from discovering the survival of the childish in ourselves. In all such cases sensations of amusement are aroused by the contrast between meaning and non-meaning in a given combination of perceptions; more particularly, they remind us of the antithesis between natural human personality and the pattern which society has imposed.

It is this latter formula, I suggest, which (when added to the strong strain of sentiment or sentimentality which runs through the whole fabric of the English sense of humour) explains the curious fact that child-jokes occupy a larger space in English humorous publications than in those of any other country. It is not, of course, that the English possess a deeper affection for children than is possessed by other nations; it is rather that the English, being by nature eccentrics, have an instinctive dislike of the adult pattern of society, and that they tend, not so much to attack the pattern directly, as to seek comfort and relief in the constant representation of those unconditioned members of society (the child and the naïve) by whom and which the pattern is exposed to consoling, rather than to disturbing, criticism.

The primal, or childish, element in the English sense of humour is also manifested by the important part assumed therein by playfulness, and especially by word-play. I am not referring to those forms of verbal dexterity which produce wit, irony, or even the more elaborate types of pun and paradox; these entail a quick movement of the intelligence and have as their aim the sudden discovery of some similarity of meaning between two or more different things. I am referring rather to those forms of word-play which are based, not so much upon a similarity of meaning, as upon the fanciful association of sounds. This specifically English amusement represents a childish, and not an adult, combination of similarities.

The pleasure which the English derive from the association of sounds at a level of consciousness between sensation and perception is not, of course, to be explained solely in terms of playfulness. There remains another element, which is certainly present, but which is difficult to isolate and define. It is not some special awareness of the inconsequent or the incongruous, since neither of these is perceived; it is not exactly a sense of contrast, since the contrast, when it exists, is felt rather than thought. It is a simultaneous awareness of doubleness and singleness, occurring at the sense-of-humour level. I can best explain my meaning by a physiological analogy.

We are all familiar with the curious sensation produced when we cross the middle finger over the index finger and then pass the V-shaped aperture thus formed up and down a thin object, such as a ruler, or even up and down the nose. We then derive an impression of having two noses and at the same time only one nose. A simultaneous sensation of doubleness and singleness is thereby produced, and on the exact level of consciousness where perception and sensation mingle. An analogous effect is created by the simpler forms of English word-play; no mental effort is needed or attempted; the reaction is, if not entirely physiological, is certainly not one by which the higher cortices of the brain are affected. It is thus a primal, or infantile, reaction.

I now pass to the self-protective element in the English sense of humour. Freud was not alone in defining the sense of humour as a defence mechanism having as its main function the protection of the self against discomfort, whether arising from internal or from external sources. He contended, however, that it was the 'loftiest' variant of the defence activities which the subconscious devises. Unlike repression, the sense of humour does not seek to withdraw painful ideas from conscious attention. It seeks only to diminish their painfulness by distributing their affects. 'Humour', he writes, 'is thus a means to gain pleasure despite the painful affects which disturb it.' It thus becomes for him 'one of the highest psychic functions'.

Jean Paul Richter, who devoted much of his life to the examination of the smaller types of happiness, also stressed the protective functions of the sense of humour. Human beings, he contended, seek instinctively to defend themselves against the unhappiness caused by the contrast between the real and the ideal, between the finite and the infinite. The mystic and the idealist seek to protect themselves by concentrating upon the infinite; the realist seeks to give to the finite the validity of the infinite; but the 'practical humorist', that is the man to whom a sense of humour has become part of his attitude towards life, adopts for his protection a mood of general good-humour, which enables him to take an indulgent view both of the finite and the infinite and to see absurdity everywhere.

We can observe the English sense of humour operating as a defence mechanism against the alarming, the unfamiliar, the horrible, the dread of ridicule,

or the pain derived from intellectual and social superiority in others. When faced with the menacing, the
English take instinctive refuge in their sense of
humour. At times this escapism assumes truly heroic
proportions, as when men and women will joke together in the face of immediate physical danger. More
frequently the mechanism is applied for less noble
purposes. An attempt is made to reduce the menacing
to the level of the comic, as when Hitler was represented, not as some daemonic force intent upon our
destruction, but as a talkative little man with a mous-
tache.

The English, again, would appear to be more sensitive than are other races to the disquiet aroused by
the unfamiliar, the foreign or the strange. The devices
which their sense of humour invents to mitigate this
disquiet are numerous and self-deceptive; they often
consist of an attempt to render the unfamiliar insig-
nificant by ignoring such serious aspects as it may
possess and by concentrating upon those aspects which
diminish its mystery. The first instinctive reaction of
the English when faced with the disturbingly unfamiliar is thus the self-protective giggle. Even more
curious is their habit of indulging in *Galgenhumor* and
seeking to mitigate the effect of tragedy or horror by
exposing them to the dispersal of sardonic humour.

One may also observe the English sense of humour
functioning to protect the individual against expected
ridicule. I laugh when I make a fool of myself, not
because I am really amused, but because I wish to
forestall the laughter of others or to comfort myself
for the humiliation I have suffered. People laugh,
again, at their social or intellectual superiors, not be-

cause they really find such eminence funny, but because they seek to compensate themselves for any
feelings of diffidence which might arise. Such expressions as 'high-brow' or 'Oxford accent' are employed
with a subconscious desire to render comic, and thereby less disquieting, the cultural superiority of others;
it is only in England that jokes are constantly directed
against erudition, scholarship, professional knowledge,
or literary and artistic originality.

It is often stated that the faculty which distinguishes
the English sense of humour from other perceptions
of the ludicrous is the faculty (which they claim to
possess so pre-eminently) of being able to laugh at
themselves. It is undeniable that the English are less
sensitive than, let us say, the Germans or the Americans, to ridicule directed against their institutions,
climate, cooking, habits and foibles. To some extent
this insensitiveness arises, not from a superior sense
of humour, but from superior self-assurance, com-
placency and pride. 'Self-dispraise', remarked Dr.
Johnson, 'is often oblique self-praise.' Were their
pride really to be humbled, were their national self-
assurance really to be assailed, I do not believe that
the English would laugh any more loudly than the
Germans or the Americans. Although the individual
Englishman will often relish jokes directed against
those of his failings (such as absent-mindedness,
greediness, unpunctuality, untidiness or extravagance)
which do not diminish his essential dignity, he will
never laugh at jokes directed against failings of which
he is inwardly ashamed.

It is instructive, moreover, to observe how readily
the English will ascribe to 'bad taste' those jokes

which transgress the boundaries which national convention has set to the ludicrous. Nor can it be said that the English possess a gift of self-criticism as pungent or as authentic as that possessed by the Jews. I conclude therefore that the circumstance that the English seem to relish 'dangerless' ridicule directed against themselves, does not diminish the self-protective element in their sense of humour; they enjoy the jokes which do not happen to pierce their armour of self-assurance; once a joke becomes painful, the mechanism of self-protection is instantly applied.

I must now examine point ix in my scheme of components, namely the economising of mental and emotional effort. One of the most common defects of the English temperament is intellectual indolence. The average Englishman does not take pleasure in cerebral effort as an end in itself. He seeks constantly to spare himself that effort, and his sense of humour is one of the many mechanisms which he applies for that purpose. Obviously, all laughter is to some extent a relief from mental tension. 'The exercise of good sense', writes Henri Bergson, 'is in itself an effort; it entails work. But to be able to detach oneself from events and at the same time to perceive images, to break with logic and at the same time to gather ideas together, that is just a game, or, if you prefer it, a bout of laziness. . . . It is a relief from the effort of thinking.' The English are very fond of games.

Freud derives much satisfaction from this 'economising' function of the sense of humour. He suggests that when we are witty we are economising inhibitions; that when we are humorous we are economising feeling; that when we indulge in *Galgenhumor*

we are economising fear; and that when we laugh at
our own incompetence and humiliation we are economising anger and self-reproach. In each of these cases
we are, according to Freud, striving to achieve
euphoria—'which', he concludes characteristically, 'is
nothing but the state of a bygone time in which we
were wont to defray our psychic work with slight
expenditure. It is in fact the state of childhood in
which we did not know the comic, were incapable
of wit, and did not need humour to make us happy.'

The extent to which the English sense of humour
functions as a labour-saving device can readily be observed. The disquiet with which, as has been noticed,
the English react to the unfamiliar finds its counterpart in the extreme relief with which they greet the
familiar. It is interesting, for instance, to observe how
large a part is played in English laughter by the
factor of recognition. A music-hall audience, for instance, will respond immediately to the recognisable,
and will laugh aloud at stock jokes, repetitions, mimicry, personifications, references to food or drink, and
any allusion to the topical.

This desire to economise in mental and psychic
effort also explains the tendency of the English to
regard as comic, insincere, or pretentious anything
which they do not happen personally to understand.
Apart from the self-protective element in such laughter
there is also the instinct to dismiss as unimportant any
subject which requires for its understanding concentrated mental effort. This inclination to ridicule the
difficult can be observed in the normal reaction of the
Englishman to innovations in art, literature and even
politics. It can also be noticed in his hatred of con-

ceptual logic, a hatred which finds an outlet in the strangest of all the many manifestations of the English sense of humour, namely the national love of nonsense.

Monsieur Emile Cammaerts, in his illuminating work *The Poetry of Nonsense*, has contended that the sense of humour 'with the meaning the English attach to it' is unique in the world. It is true that the appreciation of nonsense at least is a phenomenon which can rarely be found except among the English people. The Germans do, it is true, possess some conception of nonsense, but for pure nonsense, or nonsense for nonsense's sake, one must consult the English authors. Nonsense is in its essence a rebellion against the authority of orderly thinking; it is a war of liberation waged against conceptual logic; it is the supreme release from the constraint of reason. And if, as Bergson says, sense means work, then nonsense assuredly means play. It is in nonsense that the childishness, the play-aptitudes, the fancy and the mental indolence of the English find their most welcome outlets and excuse. The humiliation of logic fills the English, even the most erudite English, with unmixed delight; but in countries where logic is reverenced, and reason esteemed, the love of nonsense appears primal, infantile, and below the dignity of the developed man. I have found it difficult, very difficult indeed, to persuade my French friends to like Edward Lear. The English must be content to enjoy their nonsense as something intimate and private; among themselves.

I have sought, in advancing these suggestions regarding the nature and composition of the English sense of humour, to adopt a wholly objective attitude and to place myself in the position almost of a foreign observer, scrutinising something which he cannot hope to possess. I should wish, before passing to the concluding and inductive stage of my argument—before, that is, I produce my illustrations and exhibits—to conclude on a less aloof note. It has often been contended that the sense of humour, in that it aims at the provision of self-deceptive comfort, is not a reputable faculty, and is one never associated with very good or formidable men. Goethe, whose attitude to such indulgences was Olympian rather than humane, regarded a sense of humour as an evasion of manly duty. 'One cannot', he remarked to Müller, 'have a sense of humour unless one be without conscience or responsibility.' It is undoubtedly correct to say that men such as Napoleon and Hitler were immune to any sense of humour; all that they possessed was a rather savage sense of farce.

Yet it is not universally true that the sense of humour has a debilitating effect upon the character; Lincoln possessed a sense of humour and so does Winston Churchill. Nor do I agree that the English are indulging in their habitual hypocrisy when they regard their sense of humour as one of the most valuable assets which they possess. It may not be the index of a very active intellect, but it is certainly the index of a most agreeable temperament. It may be a rather childish, self-protective and indolent quality, but it is assuredly benevolent, conciliatory, kind. It may resort to devices and subterfuges which are not always very lucidly realised, but it does furnish the individual with a gyroscope which ensures the balance of his nerves. It is a lubricant in our anxious lives, an intimate and gentle friend within us, who adjusts our relation to the society in which we live, and who, when we fall among the thorns, is ever ready to bring unguents for our wounds. And above all, perhaps, it is a faculty which, in a still stratified community such as ours, remains indifferent to social and economic distinctions and almost unaffected by the harshness of class or party strife.

7

If, as I have contended, the components of the English sense of humour correspond to certain specific elements in the English temperament, then how far will my argument be confirmed or disproved by an examination of three well-known specimens of English humorous writing?

I shall begin with *Punch*. Ever since 1860 this periodical has issued a weekly ration of the sort of jokes which, in the opinion of its proprietors and editors, the English *bourgeoisie* might be expected to enjoy. I calculate (on the basis of four separate jokes to the page) that since its inception *Punch* must have emitted some 540,000 jokes: this is a formidable total. I shall exclude from my analysis the period between 1841 and 1860, since during the first nineteen years of its existence *Punch* was a satirical publication which devoted its space to attacks upon the existing order, the propertied classes, the Catholic Church and the Royal Family.

In the later 'fifties the influence of Douglas Jerrold, whom Thackeray described as 'that savage little Robespierre', began to decline; the proprietor, William Bradbury (who, as Mr. Spielmann has remarked, 'was the keenest man of business who ever trod the flags

of Fleet Street') and the editor, Mark Lemon, who had
Jewish blood, decided that it would prove more profitable to comfort the *bourgeois* than to insult them. Thus
Punch, who had not started life as a gentleman and
whose daughter in 1841 had been 'in service', decided
to become an ornament in polite, and especially in
sporting, society. By the 'seventies we find Ruskin
describing him as 'a polite Whig . . . who holds up for
the general idea of perfection, to be arrived at by all
the children of heaven and earth, the British hunting
squire, the British colonel, and the British sailor'.

Punch had from the first decided to be clean; he
would abstain, he proclaimed, 'from the unsavoury
subjects which form the principal stock in trade of
the French humorist.' He decided also to be kind, and
as the years passed his political cartoons ceased to be
caricatures and became, in the hands of Bernard Part-
ridge and others, flattering pen-and-ink portraits of
contemporary statesmen. This general tone has been
maintained with profitable consistency. *Punch* remained benevolent, humanitarian, patriotic, sentimental, fanciful, and urbane. For a hundred years
he has derided all forms of pretension and all forms
of rigidity; he must have made some 100,000 jokes
about lawyers, civil servants, doctors and dentists; he
has employed all the familiar devices of amusement
from 'sudden glory' (*e.g.* British sturdiness as con-
trasted with Continental frivolity) to automatism as opposed to free activity: he has exploited with skill, either
the denial of expectation (as in Fougasse) or the expenditure of unnecessary effort (as in Heath Robinson);
and through it all he has remained a welcome
Wednesday visitor in countless English homes.

quote the following sample from a recent issue: 'It is suggested in some quarters that Uno's motto for the moment should be "Let Azerbaijans be baijans".'

(2) SELF-PROTECTION

(a) *Against the unfamiliar*

Even in the early days *Punch* devoted much space to ridiculing the unfamiliar. He derided photography, vegetarianism, hats, crinolines, Wagner and the polka. The Suez Canal, to *Punch*, became 'that impossible trench which Mr. Lesseps pretends to think he can cut through the Isthmus of Suez'. The air was, for *Punch*, 'the last place we should look for the means of carrying on hostilities.' Ironclads were 'ferreous freaks' which 'were made in foundries and are sure to founder'. The introduction of the motor-car provided the contributors to *Punch* with almost inexhaustible material.

(b) *Against foreigners*

The tendency of *Punch* to protect the community against contamination by foreign tribes is a recurrent tendency. Foreigners are represented as volatile, boastful, frivolous, and unsturdy; they are by nature ridiculous, since they cannot speak our language, do not play our games, and are apt to use incorrect terms when referring to hunting or golf.

(*c*) *Against the alarming*

Punch has always sought to console his readers by representing the menacing as ridiculous. The jokes which he at first made about the Indian Mutiny, the Fenians, the Boers, and the Emperor William II, find their echo in the famous cartoon which was published to celebrate the Ides of March 1939.

(*d*) *Against intellectual superiority*

Punch has always pleased his readers by deriding intellectuals. The old jokes about Mrs. Cimabue Brown are echoed in 1930 by: 'An owl is said to haunt a tree in Bloomsbury; but we shall not early be persuaded that it gives two hoots for any member of the local intelligentzia.' Art, in *Punch's* view, should be representative. In 1844 we find him scoffing at Turner's 'Whalers' on the ground that 'it embodies one of those singular effects which are only met with in lobster salads and this artist's pictures'. The Pre-Raphaelites, to *Punch*, were 'dear silly boys', but when Millais painted 'The Order of Release' he was praised by *Punch* for having at last discarded his early affectations.

(3) ECONOMY OF MENTAL EFFORT

(*a*) *Love of the familiar*

The love of the familiar is the counterpart of hatred of the unfamiliar; its aim is less that of protection than of the avoidance of effort. Apart from his indulgence in the topical we can observe in *Punch* all the accustomed devices for the exploitation of the recognisable. The constant use of serials, from the 'Boompje Papers', through the serials of du Maurier, to the 'Changing Face of Britain', provides, by the device of repetition, the pleasure of rediscovering the familiar.

(b) *Making fun of knowledge*

Punch has always been inclined to regard scholarship, erudition, the expert and the mental effort they imply, as comic objects. Even his own reviewers are referred to slightingly as 'Mr. Punch's staff of learned clerks'.

(c) *Nonsense*

Only in recent years, with the arrival of Emett and J. L. Arthur, has *Punch* intentionally indulged in nonsense. It may be that, until his second childhood came upon him, he felt that nonsense would be inconsistent with the paternal dignity he had assumed.

(4) COMFORT

The above analysis suggests that one of the main purposes of *Punch* is to flatter and console his subscribers. A cartoon for January 1880 might be taken as a statement of policy. The new year is represented as an infant gazing up at a recumbent female figure. 'Please, dear Hope,' remarks the child, 'please *do* tell me a flattering tale.'

There is one device which *Punch* has always employed and which merits attention since it is not often met with in other publications. It is the transposition of modern problems into ancient terms. Sometimes this device assumes archaeological form, as in 'The Tablets of Azit-Tigleth-Miphansi', or in the comments on democracy ascribed to the Assyrian King Beliaches. Sometimes the transposition is less elaborate as in the numerous drawings by Morrow or in such jokes as 'Bread rationing in ancient Rome' or 'I see that Pompeii had it last night.' Why should this form of humour arouse sensations of amusement in English readers? Partly, of course, because it treats the stream of history as if it were a machine which could be reversed; partly because it creates a contrast between the ancient and the modern, between the unfamiliar and the familiar; partly because it implies derision of erudition; partly because it furnishes an occasion for word-play and picture-play; but mainly because it suggests the comforting thought that our present problems are not unique or catastrophic since other ages have coped with similar difficulties. The central purpose of such devices is the provision of comfort.

Although *Punch* is the main emporium from which can be obtained countless samples of the jokes which are supposed to appeal to the English sense of humour, further illustrations must be drawn from the area of nonsense which, as has been seen, is an English speciality. Two nineteenth-century pioneers of nonsense were Edward Lear and C. L. Dodgson, who wrote under the pseudonym of 'Lewis Carroll'. They each flourished under the full pressure of Victorian conventionality and each of them possessed a precise intelligence. Lear's paintings display the utmost accuracy of execution; and Dodgson was by profession a mathematician, whose *Treatise on Determinants* was published two years after *Alice's Adventures in Wonderland*.

Lear contended that his sole purpose was to arouse 'innocent mirth' by the indulgence in nonsense 'pure and absolute'. Yet if we examine his *Book of Nonsense* and *More Nonsense* we find that his humour does in fact fall into many of the patterns which we have already considered.

The pleasure of recognition, for instance, is provided by the easy jingle of his verse, and by the constant repetition in the last line of the place-names introduced into the first line. The laughter excited by the deformities of others can be found in Lear's unending references to abnormal chins, noses, mouths and ears. The amusement which the English derive from understatement is satisfied by the bland manner in which Lear's characters accept the misfortunes which fall upon them. The indulgence in word-play assumes the form of assonances, such as 'Messina-Opsibeena' or the invention of nonsense words such as 'ombliferous' and 'scroobious'

It is interesting to observe, moreover, how large a space is occupied in Lear's verses by *Galgenhumor* or the bright account of tragedy and sudden death. The mortality among Lear's characters, although fortunately the majority of them were of foreign origin, is high. A girl at Smyrna is burnt to death (or almost burnt to death) by her own grandmother; a Norwegian girl is crushed in a door; a Czechoslovak citizen contracts the plague; a Peruvian is thrust into a stove by his wife and a similar fate overcomes a Prussian; an inhabitant of Cromer falls off a cliff and a citizen of Calcutta is choked to death; an unnamed oriental dies of remorse on observing the gluttony of his children; a young Irish lady is devoured by a bear; an elderly man at Chester is stoned by children; a maiden at Janina has her head blown off; an old lady at Stroud commits mass murder; and two citizens, respectively of Ems and Cadiz, meet their death by drowning.

The popularity of Lear's verses confirms the suggestion made above that the main pleasure to be derived from nonsense is the release of the individual, either from the contemporary social pattern, or from the discipline of logical thought. Lear's characters are engaged in constant warfare with the social pattern; society, for him, is represented by 'They'. The attitude which 'They' adopt to the asocial individual is always unimaginative and often cruel. In general, Lear's characters display little resentment at the treatment meted out to them. There are moments, however, when they turn upon their tormentors. People like the man in the plum-coloured vest, the Italian woman who came from Parma, and the young lady in blue, refuse to sacrifice their individuality to any social pattern; and a similar defence of human personality was effectively championed at Sestri:

> *'There was an old person of Sestri,*
> *Who sate himself down in the vestry.*
> *When they said "You are wrong!"*
> *He merely said "Bong!"*
> *That repulsive old person of Sestri.'*

It could be contended, of course, that Lear's verses are not 'pure' nonsense, even as the Alice books are not 'pure' nonsense, since they imply a criticism of those to whom social convention seems important. Lewis Carroll's *Hunting of the Snark* and the *Lay of the Jabberwock* represent 'pure' nonsense since they possessed no purpose at all, unless it was to puzzle future psycho-analysts or to convey a pleasing sense of release from the constraints of reality.

A more contemporary illustration of the English love of nonsense is provided by the ingenious scripts which Mr. Kavanagh writes for 'Itma'. One can recognise in the 'Itma' performances almost every occasion of laughter which I have examined in this essay. They are packed with descending incongruities, denials of expectation, releases from constraint, and automatisms contrasting with free activities; they exploit the naïve-comic, absent-mindedness, all forms of rigidity or pretension, self-importance, and professionalism; they provide a constant recurrence of the inconsequent. They possess certain qualities moreover which render them specifically English. They are good-humoured, kindly, optimistic, and contain little that is malicious or offensive. And they are comforting, in that they suggest feelings of inferiority to nobody except to colonels and foreigners.

All the devices of recognition are skilfully employed. Much play is made with such readily recognisable subjects as food or beer. The topical is ingeniously woven into the whole pattern; and the element of repetition is furnished, partly by the recurrence of stock characters, and partly by the free employment of alliteration.

It is his use of word-play which gives Mr. Kavanagh a deserved place among the English humorists. There is the play on a familiar phrase: 'I never heard', exclaims Diana, 'of a scheme so foolhardy.' 'Kiss me, fool Hardy,' is the reply. There is the ordinary pun, such as 'The white man's Burton'. There is the play of pure nonsense, in which sound associations are fancifully combined:

> *Hugh*:   The Lesser Tittiwiffica.
> *Tommy*: No, it's the pretty bit of stuffica. Have a peepica? You're too late; it's flown into a taxica.

At other times Signor So-So is brought in to misuse the English language. And sometimes the word-play takes the form of a simple misconception, as when 'settlers' are mistaken for 'setters', or the following excellent dialogue occurs:

> *Tommy*: It does not pay anyone to dress shabbily.
> *Colonel*: Chablis, sir? A glorious wine! I don't mind if I do.

The 'Itma' performances provide an admirable exhibit of the English sense of humour. They operate at the level of consciousness which combines the upper grades of sensation with the lower grades of perception. They are sufficiently rapid to demand alert attention; this results in satisfied self-esteem. Yet they are not so difficult as to necessitate active intellectual effort; that might result in self-reproach.

It is said that 'Itma' is listened to by twenty million people; this is an encouraging circumstance. I am happy to conclude my essay upon so popular a note.

II

THE HEALTH OF AUTHORS

I have had the good fortune to know, and some-times to know intimately, many of the leading writers of my own country and of other countries. All I can hope to do is to lay before you, as simply as I can, the results of this experience.

So much for the problem of audience. What about the problem of subject? The title of this lecture con-tains, as you will have observed, two operative words, namely 'health' and 'authors'. I shall not trouble you much with the physical health of famous writers, except in so far as I shall seek to disprove the popular fallacy that all mighty poets must be of an ailing con-stitution and doomed to an untimely death. I shall be concerned rather with the mental health of authors and more specifically with that form of nervous activity, or sensibility, which enables its possessor to receive,—if I may beg the question for a moment,— 'intimation' and 'inspiration'. In other words I shall seek to examine how the mind of the creative writer works.

In what sense again, to complete these introductory definitions, shall I be using the word 'author'? We all tend, when viewing from outside the members of any calling or profession, to regard them as constituting a uniform category or type. I am aware, for instance, that I myself am inclined to regard lawyers as a type, or soldiers as a type, or sailors as a type. They also, I am quite sure, regard all writers, whether they be creative writers or hack writers, as more or less uniform, as the almost indistinguishable components of a small eccentric clan. Yet although the prolonged pursuit of any calling is undoubtedly apt to impose a certain uniformity of mode, manner, speech and even countenance, the members of such a calling,—how-little doubt that, in the nineteenth century at least, a high proportion of creative geniuses (and the names of Keats and the Brontës occur to one immediately) succumbed to tuberculosis. Yet if one examines objectively the mortality statistics of eminent writers one does not find that their bodily, as distinct from their mental, health (and I am aware that this is a dangerous distinction)—one does not find, I say, that their bodily health was any worse than that of their illiterate contemporaries. If, for instance, one takes a list of the thirty-two most famous British poets who flourished between the middle of the fourteenth century and the end of the nineteenth, one is struck by the fact that, given the contemporary expectation of life, they were remarkable for their longevity. Of these thirty-two famous poets as many as ten lived beyond the age of seventy, nine died between the ages of sixty and seventy, seven between the ages of fifty and sixty, two between the ages of forty and fifty, and only four under the age of forty. Nor should we forget that many of these mighty poets did not, during their lifetime, take that care of their health which their medical advisers would have recommended. Ben Jonson and Michael Drayton, as we know, were of a convivial disposition, and in fact some authorities have attributed Shakespeare's final illness to the effects of their uproarious visit to Stratford a few weeks before his death. Yet Ben Jonson lived to the then ripe age of sixty-four and Michael Drayton to the age of sixty-eight. Herrick was not particularly austere, yet he reached the most respectable age of eighty three. Swift and Dr. Johnson during their lifetime were tortured with the dread of premature decay, yet Swift retained his bodily health at least until the age of seventy-seven, and Johnson was seventy-five at the time of his death. Tennyson again, who during his middle life was a confirmed hypochondriac, lived to the venerable age of eighty-three; and Swinburne, whose early manhood was not distinguished by any pronounced asceticism, lingered on at Putney until his seventy-third year. I doubt whether if one examined the lives of thirty-two famous clergymen, lawyers or merchants between the thirteenth and the nineteenth centuries one would find that they could show an equally high average of survival.

And what of the four mighty poets who did in fact suffer an untimely death? Keats, it is true, died of consumption in Rome at the age of twenty-six; but the deaths of Marlowe and Shelley were due, not to health, but to accident. Marlowe was killed at the age of twenty-nine in a tavern brawl at Deptford; and Shelley at the age of twenty-nine was drowned in a squall off Viareggio.

There are those who contend that the fourth of these premature deaths, the death of Byron at the age of thirty-six, was also due to an accident. Such people aver that, but for the incompetence of the local doctors at Missolonghi, Byron would have survived to a reputable and perhaps repentant old age. This assertion is to my mind an unfair reflection upon the professional skill of Doctors Bruno and Van Millingen. As I have devoted much study to the last illness of Byron, and as it still constitutes one of the unsolved medical mysteries of literary history, you will perhaps allow me, in fairness to his much abused doctors, to digress outrageously for a moment and to examine the facts of the Byron case.

According to the accepted story, Byron died of a rheumatic fever at Missolonghi, induced by rowing in an open boat across the lagoon after being heated by riding and drenched by a thunderstorm. His doctors are accused of having failed to diagnose his illness and of having bled him to death. The facts do not confirm this theory. People forget to mention that on February 15, 1824, three months before his death, Byron was struck down by a convulsive fit, which he himself, perhaps incorrectly, assumed to be epileptic. On the advice of Major Parry, he treated himself for this affliction by drinking enormous quantities of cider laced with strong insertions of brandy: I cannot believe that in the paludal climate of Missolonghi that was a wise thing to do. It is quite true that in April he was drenched in a thunderstorm and that two days later he went out riding on a saddle which was still wet. Yet if his ten days' illness, which lasted from April 9 to April 19, was in fact rheumatic fever it is strange that he did not suffer the intense pain associated with that illness and even more strange that he was able on April 14 to walk unassisted from one room to the other. Nor is there any mention in the many accounts of his illness either of the heavy perspiration or of the swelling joints which rheumatic fever, as I understand, invariably produces. I am advised indeed by those experts whom I have consulted, that Byron's final illness must have been either typhoid or pernicious malaria.

And what about the famous accusation that Drs. Bruno and Van Millingen bled their patient to death? They may have wished to bleed him copiously, but they did not succeed. Obstinately he refused to be bled until almost the last moment, remarking, perhaps not inappropriately, to Dr. Bruno that 'the lancet, as he well knew, had killed more people than the lance'. It was only on the 16th of April, three days before his death, that he at last consented to be bled. According to Dr. Van Millingen's account he stretched out his arm with the angry words 'Come; you are, I see, a damned set of butchers; take away as much blood as you will; but have done with it'. This is confirmed exactly in Dr. Bruno's account, who records him as 'prestando il braccio in una maniera disgustosa'. They then drew a full pound of blood but the fever did not, to their surprise, subside for long. It may well be that, in his then condition, a pound of blood was an excessive quantity to have drawn; but I am assured that in so doing Byron's doctors were in no way violating the conventions of their age. And I doubt whether, even if, as was hoped at one time, an English doctor could have reached him from the garrison at Zante or Corfu, this consultant would have made any very different diagnosis or have prescribed any very different treatment. The death of Byron was undoubtedly a misfortune, but we should be unfair to Drs. Bruno and Van Millingen, were we to perpetuate the legend that it was also an accident.

In any case I have, I suggest, said enough to indicate that the bodily health of authors, if I may venture such an expression, is as sound as that of the members of any other calling. I must now pass to the more interesting consideration of their mental health, or, as I should prefer to phrase it in less controversial terms, to a consideration of the literary temperament.

3

The theory that there exists some special connection between literary genius and mental derangement is one which, to my mind, has been much exaggerated. It is true that a few creative writers have in their later years become demonstrably insane; it is also true that almost all creative writers have at some moments of their lives been panic-stricken by the conviction that their imagination was getting the better of their reason; but it is not in the least true that *all* creative writers have been mad *all* the time.

I must admit that the authorities for this distressing theory are both honourable and ancient. Plato contended that there were two forms of what he called delirium, namely insanity and inspiration. 'I have observed this about poets,' he writes in the *Apology*. 'It is not by taking thought that they create what they create; it is owing to a natural disposition and when ecstatically possessed.' Burton, in the *Anatomy of Melancholy* gives us the short sharp phrase 'All poets are mad'. Shakespeare assures us that

> *'The lunatic, the lover and the poet,*
> *Are of imagination all compact',*

he speaks of the 'poet's eye, in a fine frenzy rolling'; and in the less familiar conclusion to this famous passage he gives us the following suggestive lines:

> *'Such tricks hath strong imagination,*
> *That, if it would but apprehend some joy,*
> *It comprehends some bringer of that joy;*
> *Or in the night, imagining some fear,*
> *How easy is a bush supposed a bear!'*

Dryden in *Absalom and Achitophel* gave popular currency to this idea in his perhaps too well-known couplet:

'Great wits are sure to madness near allied;
And thin partitions do their bounds divide.'

Macaulay goes so far as to say 'perhaps no person can be a poet, or can even enjoy poetry, without a certain unsoundness of mind'. And Lamartine speaks of 'that mental malady which men call genius'.

I could, if I so desired, extend by any number of quotations the comments which writers have passed upon their own mental derangement. I have quoted enough however to establish the point that writers are themselves largely to blame if the public regard them as unbalanced. In their lack of reticence, in their self-conscious habit of examining their nerves in public, it is they, rather than the outsiders, who have created the legend of their instability.

Yet the legend persists. As an example of the lengths to which it can be pushed I should refer to Mr. J. F. Nesbit's well known book entitled *The Insanity of Genius*, which was published in 1891, and which every year since then has caused a great amount of pain to a large number of people. 'Genius and insanity', writes Mr. Nesbit, 'are in reality different phases of morbid susceptibility of, or want of balance in, the cerebro-spinal system.' In the strictly medical sense this may, for all I know, be true; but it is distressing for a creative writer, and disturbing for his family and descendants, to be told that what he and they believed to be a glorious boon from Apollo is in fact no more than a diseased condition of what I understand is called the *medulla oblongata.* Mr. Nesbit, moreover, although from time to time he will let fall a word or two of comfort, examined the case histories and the family histories of distinguished writers with sadistic glee. If the grandfather or grandmother of an author can be shown to have possessed a weak chest or a tendency to rheumatism, their unhappy grandchild is accused by Mr. Nesbit of being congenitally neurotic. I am not exaggerating. Let me quote the relevant passage from Mr. Nesbit's cruel work. 'Genius,' he writes, 'insanity, idiocy, scrofula, rickets, gout, consumption and other members of the neuropathetic family of disorders, are so many different expressions of a common evil—an instability, or want of equilibrium, in the nervous system.' I am not saying that, in a technical sense, this may not all be true; but surely if one applied similar all-embracing tests to the case histories and the family histories of civil servants, bankers, postmen and even aviators, one would arrive at a closely similar result. To contend that a man is liable to mental derangement merely because his uncle suffered from gout is to advance a contention which, you will agree, is palpably absurd. Of course all creative writers are nervous; even Horace, that complacent hedonist, referred to them as the *'genus irritabile vatum'*—'that tetchy breed of bards'; but to be nervous, even to be extremely nervous, does not necessarily imply that one is suffering from a nervous disease.

It is for these reasons that I reject the extreme imputation which is suggested by Dryden's couplet and which has been expanded in Mr. Nesbit's long, and I must admit extremely interesting, book. But it is not enough merely to reject the imputation. I must examine the evidence and make at least some suggestions as to how, even in the minds of creative writers themselves, the legend has arisen.

4

A few eminent writers have, it must be admitted, relapsed in their later years into a state of idiocy. Others must honestly be described as 'border-line cases'. And almost all creative writers have been convinced at one time or another that they were about to lose the control of their own brain.

Yet of the thirty-two famous British poets whose longevity I commended at the outset of this lecture, only two became demonstrably insane. Swift throughout his life was haunted by the spectre of insanity. 'I shall be like that tree,' he once said to a friend, indicating a decaying elm, 'I shall die at the top.' Yet Swift in fact lived to the age of seventy-seven and it was only in the last three years of his life that his intellect became clouded. William Cowper, the 'stricken deer' of Lord David Cecil's beautiful biography, was subjected from his twenty-first year to recurrent fits of melancholia and suicidal mania. Twice in his life he almost succeeded in hanging himself and was only saved by chance. Yet although Cowper had twice to be placed in confinement, or at least under supervision, he enjoyed long interludes of perfect sanity, during which he composed much excellent poetry and was happy in a quiet tea-party sort of way. It cannot be said that Cowper was ever a demented maniac; the worst that could be said of him was that he was sometimes sadly confused in the head.

Dr. Johnson might, I suppose, be regarded (and

would certainly be so regarded by Mr. Nesbit), as a border-line case. He suffered at times from auditory hallucinations and he cherished many strange delusions such as his belief that he would get drunk if he ate an apple. He was, poor man, obsessed by the dread of losing his wits. 'Insanity', records Boswell, 'was the object of his most dismal apprehension, and he fancied himself seized by it, or approaching to it, at the very time when he was giving proofs of more than ordinary soundness and vigour of judgement.' There is no evidence that this dread was anything more than one of Dr. Johnson's many harmless delusions. But he certainly pushed it far. He entrusted his secret to Mrs. Thrale, and whenever he felt that madness was approaching, he would persuade her to lock him in his room and it seems to place gyves upon his legs, and even to whip him with a rod. Certain obscure references in Mrs. Thrale's journal and letters, and in the Doctor's own diary, can only be interpreted in this sense. But although Johnson was unhappily convinced of his own impending mental collapse he in fact retained his sanity to the very end. He died of asthma and dropsy at the age of seventy-five.

To these border-line cases Mr. Nesbit would I suppose add that of Southey. It is true that in his sixty-eighth year Southey's mind became clouded twelve months before his death. It is true also that Carlyle, after a visit from Southey, exclaimed 'how has this man contrived, with such a nervous system, to keep alive for near sixty years?' But there is no real evidence to suggest that Southey, except during the last twelve months, was anything but certifiably sane.

If therefore, out of my thirty-two famous British

poets, only two can be described as definitely mad, and only one can with justice be classified as a border-line case, how comes it that the legend of mental illness among creative writers has been so persistent? That, I repeat, is to a very large extent the fault of the writers themselves. All writers, and especially all poets, feel it dull to be thought completely normal. They thus divulge and even display their eccentrici-ties. Nor should I deny that these eccentricities exist. Let me give you the example of Shelley.

I should describe Shelley as on the whole a sane and normal person. One has only to read his *Defence of Poetry*, or his *Julian and Maddalo* to realise how stable, except in moments of excitement, was the poise of his mind. Yet from his childhood Shelley had possessed what his mother would have described as 'a highly strung nature' and the passionate rages into which he was thrown by being bullied at Eton caused him to be known by his school-fellows as 'mad Shelley'. The facility with which English schoolboys attribute in-sanity to anyone who is not perfectly attuned to their own herd behaviour has always struck me as curious and distressing. Shelley was certainly not mad; but he was eccentric, and his eccentricity took two par-ticular forms.

In the first place he was a hypochondriac. All creative writers are hypochondriacs, since those of them who do not worry about the state of their bodies are certain to worry about the state of their minds. Shelley, having little gift of self-criticism, seldom regarded himself as mentally afflicted, but he persistently regarded himself as very very ill. Hogg speaks of his 'unfounded frights and dislikes, his vain apprehensions and terrors'. It was no comfort to him that his doctors, and even his money-lenders, insisted that his was a thoroughly good life in the insurance sense of that term. He was convinced that he was consumptive and entering upon a decline. Even when consumption ceased to obsess him he would invent fresh diseases with which to lacerate his anxieties. On one occasion he found himself in a crowded stage-coach opposite a lady whose legs were unusually distended. He had recently been reading a book of travels in which there was a description of the disease known as elephantiasis or Barbados leg. He jumped to the conclusion that this disease must be contagious and that he had caught it from the lady with thick legs in the coach. Within a few hours he observed upon his hands the symptoms of cracked and roughened skin which, as he had read, were the presages of this dire disease. Two days later, while sitting in an arm-chair talking to Mr. and Mrs. Newton, he fell writhing upon the carpet. His hostess, in pardonable anxiety, asked him what was wrong. He informed her, still writhing, that he had been assailed with a sudden and acute attack of elephantiasis. And, according to the testimony of both Hogg and Peacock, he persisted in this unhappy delusion for several weeks.

The second form assumed by Shelley's eccentricity was that of spectral and auditory hallucinations. It is customary for every gifted writer to see spectres and to hear voices calling. After all, even Goethe (who assuredly was a man of the most Olympian calm and sanity), once met himself riding along a road on horse-back. Shelley's hallucinations were vivid and detailed. On one occasion, while walking near Pisa, he saw a man coming slowly towards him dressed in a long cloak and with a hood or cowl hiding his face. When the man was only a few yards distant he raised his hood, and Shelley was much startled to see that the man was in fact himself. The spectre then addressed a question to him in the Italian language. '*Siete sodisfatto?*' it asked him, 'Are you satisfied?' At which the spectre vanished or passed on. On another occasion, at Lerici, Shelley saw a baby rise from the sea and clap its hands at him. These are in so far as I know, the only two recorded instances, apart from the Welsh bogey, of Shelley's hallucinations; but it is evident from the writings of his friends that these sounds and visions were of not infrequent occurrence. And yet Shelley, I repeat, was certainly not mad.

If one is to account for these departures from reality, one can only do so by considering in what manner creative writers, and especially poets, are inspired. Inspiration is a sudden flash or fusion between sense and fantasy, between reason and imagination. It is generally both a confusing and an exhausting episode, and one which often leaves behind it a bruise in the mind. 'Such tricks', wrote the greatest of all poets in the passages I quoted earlier, 'Such tricks hath strong imagination.' I now propose, in my concluding sections, to make some reflections upon the nature of inspiration such as will, I trust, convince you that the illusions,—or if you like, the hallucinations—of creative writers are not grave symptoms of mental alienation but merely the tricks which a strong imagination is all too apt to play.

5

I stated at the outset of this lecture that it would be an error to regard all authors, or even all creative writers, as constituting a uniform category or type. They are in fact multiform. Even in their methods, their hours and their habits of work they display an astonishing diversity.

There are those, for instance, who possess the intense powers of concentration so startlingly manifested by Archimedes and who would agree with Newton, and also with Thomas Edison, that all creative thought is due to 'patient attention'. Such writers, and Wordsworth was one of them, can only bring their work to completion by agonised plodding along a single road. Others prefer a constant variation of theme. Thus Jane Austen kept *Sense and Sensibility*, *Pride and Prejudice*, and *Mansfield Park* upon her desk in various stages of completion, and would flit from one to the other. Burns and Beethoven were often engaged upon two or three themes at the same moment. And de Musset expressed the view that it was good for the mind to have a 'two-fold exercise'.

Some geniuses can only begin to write in the silent privacy of their own studies and to them even a blackbird calling becomes a person from Porlock. Others are actually stimulated by interruptions. Thackeray found that his ideas flowed more freely in the congested, if somnolent, atmosphere of the Athenaeum Club. Mozart actually preferred when composing to be surrounded by the hum of general conversation, in which, incredible as it may seem, he would often participate. A similar talent, so I am told, was possessed by Sidney Keyes, that gifted poet who was killed in Tunisia at the age of twenty-one. Keyes, it seems, was able to write poetry when surrounded by his undergraduate friends, and he would alternate his attention between composition of a poem and awareness of the conversation which was proceeding around him. And Schubert wrote one of his loveliest songs on the back of the bill-of-fare while sitting listening to the band in a public beer-garden.

Some authors find it more stimulating to commune with their muse in the early morning; others—such as Balzac, Byron, Dostoievsky and Conrad—could only work well at night. Some people—and I am told that Miss Edith Sitwell is one of them—write best in a recumbent position; Voltaire at Ferney did most of his dictating from his bed. For others, movement is necessary. Many writers,—and Dr. Johnson among them—have recorded that their ideas flowed more freely to the movement of a carriage or a train; Victor Hugo composed some of his loveliest lyrics when sitting on the top of an omnibus between Passy and the Bourse. Helmholtz has recorded that his mind never worked so rapidly as 'during the slow ascent of wooded hills on a sunny day'. André Gide thinks out his subject lying down and writes it standing up at a high desk. Milton asserted that he could only write really well between October and March; other writers, including Tennyson, are more often inspired during the spring and summer. Even the technical tricks and habits of authors vary enormously. Schiller found it necessary to stimulate his unconscious by keeping rotten apples in the drawer of his writing-table. Thackeray, Mme. de Staël and Southey, found that their brains would only begin to ferment if they held an actual quill or pen in their hands; and many authors of my acquaintance have confessed to me that their ideas only begin to flow easily if the objects on their writing-table are arranged in a certain pattern. There are moreover few writers who would not agree that when stuck in a passage they find it necessary to leave their table and pace rapidly around the room.

I have quoted these divergencies of method and habit in order to indicate that if there in fact exists such a thing as the literary temperament then assuredly it assumes the most diverse forms. These differences between authors in the actual practice of writing bring into sharp relief their general agreement in regard to the principle of writing, namely the nature of inspiration. Almost all writers who have ventured to express views upon this intricate matter are agreed that inspiration is an event which has no apparent connection with conscious thought. They are all agreed that it is something involuntary, spontaneous, sudden, and transitory; they are all agreed that it is something phenomenal and extraneous to the personality which receives it; and that it brings with it a sense of inevitability, naturalness, and conviction. Allow me to examine these assertions in greater detail.

6

All creative writers are agreed that inspiration,—or if you prefer the word, 'intimation'—is independent of the conscious mind. 'Poetry', writes Shelley, 'is not like reasoning—a power to be exerted according to the determination of the will.' 'It won't come', says Byron more simply 'when called.' For Byron in fact inspiration was invariably a verbal impulse; he was incapable of that plodding assiduity which Wordsworth and A. E. Housman displayed. 'I can never re-cast anything,' he wrote to Thomas Moore, 'I am like a tiger; if I miss the first spring, I go back grumbling to my jungle again.' All poets, and I regard them as the true exhibits of the creative writer, are thus agreed that inspiration can by no means be commanded. 'It comes', said Thomas Gray, 'as the maggot bites.'

Inspiration, moreover, is not only extraneous to the person experiencing it, but it is also irresistible; the victim feels himself to be possessed. 'It seems', wrote Thackeray, 'as if some occult power were moving my pen.' This feeling,—which is common to all writers and not confined only to poets—accounts doubtless for the personification of the nine muses and for the frequent references which we find in the confessions of authors to their ministering spirit or 'daimon'. It is a further proof of its assumed extraneous quality.

Poets and writers also refer to the 'inevitability' of inspiration and to its utter naturalness. 'If poetry', wrote Keats, 'come not as naturally as the leaves to the tree, it had better not come at all.' There is a story of Blake, when shown by Constable a drawing of fir trees, exclaiming 'But this is not drawing: this is inspiration'. 'I never knew that before,' answered Constable, 'I meant it for drawing.'

Several creative writers have asserted that inspiration comes to them more frequently when they are feeling unwell. 'I have seldom written poetry', confessed A. E. Housman, 'unless I was rather out of health.' André Gide modified this extreme statement.

Among the conditions of inspiration that he analyses he included: 'To feel well after having been ill.'

Even more interesting is the almost universal insistence among poets and creative writers upon the transitory nature of all these sudden intimations and inspirations. 'The mind in creation', wrote Shelley—and the idea has seldom been better expressed;—'The mind in creation is as a fading coal, which some invisible influence, like an inconstant wind, awakens to transitory brightness. Could this influence be durable in its original purity and force it is impossible to predict the greatness of the results; but when composition begins, inspiration is already on the decline.' The same idea echoes in the tragic stanza in which Carducci concluded his *Canto dell'Amore*: 'Alas! I had heard one note of the eternal poem. And what is this? Just a tiny little verse.' (*e picciol' verso or è.*) All writers are conscious of the transitory nature of these sudden intimations; some of them take precautions to capture the butterfly before it flits away. Philip Sidney, Rossetti and Tennyson always carried note-books in their pockets; Thomas Hardy would scribble phrases or ideas that came to him suddenly upon the bark of a tree when walking; and Thomas Hobbes used to keep writing materials attached to his walking-stick in order to take notes 'immediately a thought darted'.

Almost universal also is the sense of loneliness, abandonment, failure and pathetic incompetence which assails creative writers when the fleeting intimation has passed by. Some of them complain bitterly that their muse has left them for ever and that they will never be able to write again. Some of them resort to stimulants, opiates or narcotics. Others do not believe believing that they have during their dreams composed a masterpiece, the verses thus suggested prove, if written down, to be complete nonsense. Cerebration therefore ought not to be quite so unconscious as all that. Mrs. Gaskell in her admirable biography tells us that Charlotte Brontë would often moon about for weeks and even months without being able to put pen to paper. And then suddenly one morning 'the progress of her tale lay clear and bright before her'. Perhaps the most deliberate and cheerful practitioner of the method of unconscious cerebration was Sir Walter Scott. He always claimed that the half hour between waking and rising was for him the most propitious moment for composition. 'This is so much the case', he wrote, 'that I am in the habit of relying upon it, and saying to myself when at a loss, "Never mind! We shall have it at seven o'clock to-morrow morning".' Mr. Graham Wallas agrees with Sir Walter Scott in advocating unconscious cerebration as a deliberate method of, or device for, literary composition. 'In the case', he writes, 'of the more difficult forms of creative thought . . . it is desirable, not only that there should be an interval free from conscious thought on the particular problem, but also that the interval be so spent that nothing should interfere with the free working of the unconscious, or partially conscious, processes of the mind.' It was with this idea, doubtless, that the late Lord Balfour used to recommend to those of his staff who were suffering from overwork a three days' course consisting of detective novels and champagne. He would contend that by this method the blood was drawn away from the congested centres of the brain. And having on one occasion in my life been obliged to submit to, or to enjoy, this system, I am prepared to believe that both Mr. Graham Wallas and Lord Balfour were correct. Nor would any regular writer or thinker deny for a moment that the effects of subconscious cerebration are frequent, beneficial and mysterious.

7

I must now come to some conclusion. I have suggested that, in so far as concerns what as a layman I may perhaps be allowed to call 'bodily health', the author is neither more, nor less, healthy than any other sedentary individual. The creative writer, the poet and the artist do however possess a certain special nervous sensibility, which manifests itself, not merely in their receptivity to inspiration, but also in certain, apparently morbid, eccentricities. When poets and writers contend, as they so invariably do contend, that 'inspiration' reaches them from outside they are describing an experience which is in no way abnormal but perfectly natural. It is true that these sudden and transitory intimations reach them from outside the area of their consciousness; they reach them from their subconscious; there is no need at all to drag in the supernatural phenomena of muses and daimons. Genius, in spite of Buffon and Carlyle, is not either a 'great aptitude for patience' or 'a transcendant capacity for taking trouble'. It is a *spontaneous* activity of the cells and fibres of the brain whereby new combinations of impressions are constantly being formed. In insanity, as Mr. Nesbit has remarked, the nerve-connections which should enable an individual to remain in touch with his surroundings are weakened or destroyed; in genius these connections remain intact. Yet there does often occur, in moments of inspiration or intense creative activity, some flooding of the conscious by the subconscious, and therefore some dissociation from reality. This mingling or flooding may in some cases produce extreme absence of mind and even hallucinations. More usually it creates that 'trance-like state' to which W. B. Yeats referred. And almost always it produces some confusion between the imagined and the real, between the earthly life of the individual and the ideal world which he has peopled and conceived. 'Now let us talk of realities,' said Balzac to Jules Sandeau, 'let us talk about Eugénie Grandet.' It was this that Dickens meant when he said to Forster, 'I don't invent it: I see it and write it down' or when he assured Lewes that he 'actually heard every word that his characters addressed to him'. It was in this sense also that Flaubert, having described the suicide of Madame Bovary, felt a strong taste of arsenic in his mouth and was physically sick. No writer has ever composed or imagined anything of value without passing through these strange processes of identification. Yet such manifestations, I repeat, are not necessarily symptoms of morbidity; in almost every case they are as natural to an author as are the leaves to the tree.

Be sure of one thing always. All authors are not of the same value or endowed either with comparable talents or with an identic temperament. At the bottom of the scale you have those men and women who, being gifted with a certain capacity for observation and narration, can both notice and annotate the world which swims around them. Such writers are as happy and unperturbed as water-beetles jerking with long prehensile legs along the surface of the village pond. In a higher scale come the novelists who from their memories and associations construct an imaginary world of their own which to them becomes one half, and perhaps more than one half, of reality. For them imagination is a diffused and comparatively constant frame of mind and when inspiration comes to them, it comes, not as some intense and terrible visitation, but as a sudden and most welcome dissolution of an accumulated perplexity.

Raised above all others, living in a rarified ether of their own, confused by the eternal dissonance between the ideal and the real, the mighty poets are a race apart. For them imagination is no happy mood but a superb and agonised bewilderment. Not for them are the tiny pleasures, the small disappointments, the trivial success and failure, of the lesser breeds. The God visits them, not amicably, but in a flash of flame and fire; and in the after vacancy they know that they have caught but a momentary glimpse of intimation: their triumph is clouded by the knowledge that their illumination has been so narrow and so short.

Yet remember this also. No writer, however feeble he may be, can be of any value unless he possesses a powerful imagination; and powerful imaginations, as Shakespeare assures us—and he ought to know—are apt to play one tricks. Be kind, therefore, I beg you, to all authors, and above all to poets. Do not snub them when they assure you that they have caught elephantiasis from a lady in a bus; do not assume too solemn an expression when they confide to you that in Jermyn Street yesterday afternoon they met a gentleman in a tussore suit who, upon inspection, proved to be themselves; be gentle with them when they complain, as all authors have at every stage of their careers complained, that their mind and memory have crumbled and that the Muse will never visit them again. And never urge them in any circumstances to take a rest; no creative writer ever *can* take a rest; urge them only to embark upon some different sort of work, even if it be only detective novels and champagne. And remember always, I beg you, that they are seldom quite so mad as they believe; or as they seem.

III

TENNYSON'S TWO BROTHERS

III

TENNYSON'S TWO BROTHERS

I

A STRANGER, happening to ride through the village of Somersby on a Sunday morning in 1827, would have observed a procession crossing from the rectory to the small thatched church across the road. At the head of the procession stalked the rector, the Rev. George Tennyson, gaunt, sallow, enraged. The black blood which flowed in the veins of all the Tennysons had in his case turned to bile. He had been disinherited in favour of his younger brother. The promise of his early Cambridge days, the prospect of succeeding to the rich estate of Bayon's Manor, had, owing to some flicker in his father's temperament, been suddenly denied: he had been relegated to a calling for which he had little vocation, to a small and hidden parsonage among the Lincolnshire wolds. It is not surprising that the Rev. George Tennyson, afflicted as he was by one great injustice and a numerous family, should (as his more favoured brother subsequently recorded) have 'given way to feelings arising out of a nervous temperament'. Stern and melancholy, he was for long remembered in the locality as being 'amazing sharp' with his children: his brooding, angry, presence threw a shadow along the rectory walls.

Upon the rector's arm, as they walked to church, clung his gentle and long-suffering wife, Elizabeth. Behind them followed the regiment of their children. The stranger, observing this procession, would have been startled by their foreign appearance. The seven lanky sons, the four lanky daughters, followed their parents in a straggling line, clasping prayer-books in their big brown hands. First came Frederick, then a Cambridge undergraduate of twenty years of age; he was accompanied by Charles, aged nineteen, and Alfred, aged eighteen; they were followed by the sequence of their younger brothers and sisters: Mary, Emily, Edward, Arthur, Septimus, Matilda, Cecilia and Horatio. Swarthy the young men were, with long loose limbs and uncombed hair; it was as if a troop of Spaniards had irrupted suddenly into the depths of rural England. When they spoke to each other, one could detect in their hollow voices, the broad vowel-sounds of the Lincolnshire dialect.

It is with Alfred Tennyson's two elder brothers, Frederick and Charles, that this lecture will be mainly concerned. The subsequent history of the eight younger children need not long detain us. I shall refer to it only as indicating the congenital talents and eccentricities of the whole Tennyson tribe. Of the four daughters, Mary, the eldest, married Judge Ker, and their son, Walter Ker, became a competent scholar and contributed several volumes to the Loeb Classical Library. Cecilia married Edmund Lushington, of Park House, Maidstone, the scene of the Prologue to *The Princess*. Emily, having been engaged to Arthur Hallam, subsequently married Captain Richard Jesse of the Royal Navy. In her declining years she became a Swedenborgian and a spiritualist. And Matilda, who was referred to by the family as 'Tilly' developed religious melancholia and would sit for hours beside the fire sobbing over the eternal damnation of her kith and kin: she died in 1913 in her hundredth year.

Of the four younger sons there is little to record; it does not seem that their subsequent relations with their famous brother were either intimate or constant. In Burke's *Peerage* for 1890 (the proof of which must surely have been revised either by the Laureate or his son), no information is provided about them, beyond their dates of birth. Edward, who once published a sonnet in the *Yorkshire Literary Annual* was for many years kept in confinement and lived until 1890. Arthur was twice married and resided at Hampstead. Horatio, unlike the rest of the family, displayed no literary tastes whatsoever; he is reported by his nephew never to have opened a book; he desired to enter the army but was packed off to Tasmania; he married Charlotte Carey Elwes and had three children. Septimus incurred the Laureate's displeasure by mooning about the lanes of County Down dressed in a long black cape with a huge sombrero on his head. Of him is told a story which his great-niece, Miss Tennyson Jesse, assures me is authentic. Some guests, arriving early for a dinner party, were startled by a huge black man who unrolled himself slowly from the hearth rug. 'I am Septimus', he said, 'the most morbid of all the Tennysons.' There remain the two elder brothers, Frederick and Charles. About them we have much more information.

2

I have heard a story that on one occasion the Laureate was asked by a daring visitor what poetry had most influenced him in his youth. 'My own', Lord Tennyson is said to have replied, 'at the age of five.' There is no doubt that the three elder sons of the Rev. George Tennyson, Frederick, Charles and Alfred, composed verses together from their earliest years. They shared a bedroom in the rectory attic which was approached by a dark staircase from the ground floor and which possessed, in addition to the small lattice window, a skylight which has since been closed up. This room is celebrated in one of the more unfortunate of the Laureate's early poems:

> *'Oh darling room, my heart's delight,*
> *Dear room, the apple of my sight,*
> *With thy two couches [there were in*
> *   fact three couches] soft and white,*
>
> *There was no room so exquisite,*
> *No little room so warm and bright*
> *Wherein to read, wherein to write.'*

This poem (which Arthur Hallam had, with his usual impulsive adulation, pronounced to be 'mighty pleasant') was included in the 1830 volume and exposed the young Tennyson to Lockhart's scathing derision and to Bulwer's gibe about 'schoolmiss Alfred'. A later critic referred to Somersby in general, and to the attic bedroom in particular, as 'a nest of singing birds'. And it was certainly in the darling room that Alfred Tennyson, urged on by the example and encouragement of his two elder brothers, composed his earliest poems.

The result of this triple activity was a volume entitled *Poems by Two Brothers*. This volume, the manuscript of which can be seen in Trinity College Library, was published by J. and J. Jackson of Louth in the last months of 1826, although it bears the imprint of 1827. All three brothers contributed to the volume; it contains forty-eight poems by Alfred, forty-eight poems by Charles, and three by Frederick, including a long and meaningless rhapsody entitled *The Oak of The North*.

When shown this forgotten volume in his later years, the Laureate expressed astonishment at its excellent quality. He was annoyed, however, by the statement that the poems had been written when the authors were between fifteen and eighteen years of age. 'I myself', he wrote, 'had at the time done far better things. When these poems were published, Charles was eighteen. I was seventeen.'

It is seldom profitable to dissect juvenilia, nor can it be said that this collection of 1826 displays any marked precocity. Yet the volume is interesting as showing us—by its innumerable quotations, footnotes and epigraphs—what a wide and unorthodox range of books the Rev. George Tennyson allowed his sons to read.

There are twenty quotations from Horace, eight from Virgil, six from Byron, five from Isaiah, four from Ossian, three from Cicero, and two each from Moore, Xenophon, Milton, Claudian and Jeremiah. In addition, we have references to such varied writers as John Clare, Juvenal, Gibbon, Young, Apollonius Rhodius, Lucretius, Rousseau, Chapman, Spenser and Shakespeare. Frederick, it is true, had been at Eton and was at the time an undergraduate at St. John's

College, from which he was later transferred to Trinity. But Charles and Alfred, after a miserable period at the grammar school at Louth, had been educated at home; it was in their father's study that they absorbed such scholarship as they possessed. Their reading may not perhaps have been very deep; it was certainly both varied and wide.

It is curious, moreover, to examine the poems attributed to each of the three brothers and to note both the similarities and the differences. One finds, for instance, a common love of domesticity, a common preoccupation with detail, and a common absence of even the rudiments of humour. 'Oh! never', exclaims Charles Tennyson:

> *'Oh! never may frowns and dissension molest*
> *The pleasure I find at the social hearth;*
> *A pleasure the dearest—the purest—the best*
> *Of all that are found or enjoy'd on the earth!'*

Those lines, if technically better modulated, could well have been written by Alfred Tennyson in the earlier—or indeed in the later—stages of his development. The note of domesticity, the rectory parlour note, or what his enemies would call the 'schoolmiss Alfred note', was apt to recur even in the poems of his maturity. He would himself have defended and described such passages as 'tender passages'. 'Where's now', he writes at the age of sixteen or seventeen:

> *'Where's now that peace of mind*
> *O'er youth's pure bosom stealing,*
> *So sweet and so refin'd,*
> *So exquisite a feeling?'*

Such verses may be crude; but the sentiment, the sensitiveness, recur.

In seeking to deduce from *Poems by Two Brothers* the atmosphere of Somersby rectory, we notice also a foretaste of the Laureate's minute observation of nature, of his preoccupation with detail. In a contribution by Charles Tennyson we find the lines:

> '*The smallest herb or leaf can charm*
> *The man whom nature's beauties warm.*'

And here is one of Alfred Tennyson's stanzas, which (humourless and clumsy though it be) does certainly foreshadow something of his later energy of perception:

> '*The glittering fly, the wondrous things*
> *That microscopic art descries;*
> *The lion of the waste which springs*
> *Bounding upon his enemies;*
> *The mighty sea-snake of the storm,*
> *The vorticella's viewless form.*'

It is characteristic of Alfred Tennyson's unfortunate habits of precision that the word 'vorticella' is explained in a footnote. 'See', we are reminded, 'Baker on Animalculae.'

More important than these similarities are the differences which one can observe in the earliest poems of these three brothers. In Frederick's verses we notice that addiction to rhetoric which, although almost wholly meaningless, impressed Edward Fitzgerald profoundly. We also notice his uncertain handling of vowel sounds and grammar. Frederick opens one of his three contributions as follows:

> ''*Tis the voice of the dead*
> *From the depths of their glooms:*
> *Hark! they call me away*
> *To the world of the tombs.*'

Fitzgerald, it seems, enjoyed that sort of thing. He called it: 'Such gloomy grand stuff as you write.'

In Charles's poems we notice the timid appreciation of small and delicate things. He writes of 'the pensile dew-drop's twinkling gleam', of thistledown, of glow-worms. In all his later poetry we find the themes of dew and gossamer invariably recurring. And in Alfred's poems we are impressed, not merely by a metrical power far more compelling than that of his two elder brothers, not merely by his precocious aptitude in the combination of vowel-sounds, but also by a note of that gloomy mysticism which in after years produced his finest poetry. Neither Charles nor Frederick was capable of writing a stanza such as this which Alfred composed before he was seventeen:

> 'I wander in darkness and sorrow,
>   Unfriended and cold and alone,
> As dismally gurgles beside me
>   The bleak river's desolate moan,
> The rise of the volleying thunder
>   The mountain's low echoes repeat;
> The roar of the wind is around me,
>   The leaves of the year at my feet.'

Yet this lecture, I repeat, is not directly concerned with Alfred Tennyson; it is concerned with Frederick and Charles. And since, with the publication of *Poems by Two Brothers*, the three part company, I must now leave the attic bedroom of Somersby and speak, first about Frederick and thereafter about Charles: about Tennyson's two brothers.

3

There are few pastimes more agreeable than that of strolling through the byways of literature. True it is that one is obliged to traverse many arid patches and much sandy waste; but from time to time one discovers little coppices of loveliness or some strange quirk of nature which arouses interest or surprise. Of these small surprises one of the most constant is that caused by the inability, even of gifted men and women, properly to estimate the relative value of their contemporaries. Edward Fitzgerald, for instance, was a man of wide culture, sensitive literary taste and considerable critical acumen. He was one of the first to recognise and expound the genius of Blake. But when it came to balancing the merits of the three Tennyson brothers his judgement became strangely uncertain. I am not suggesting of course that Fitzgerald was unaware that Charles was a better poet than Frederick and Alfred a better poet than either. All I am suggesting is that Fitzgerald did not assess correctly the relative value of the three brothers or realise with sufficient clarity that, whereas Alfred Tennyson was among the great poets of all time, and whereas Charles Tennyson was a minor English poet of some distinction, Frederick Tennyson was little more than a rather boring eccentric with a knack of writing verse.

Fitzgerald did not know the Tennyson brothers during the Cambridge period, although he remembered seeing Alfred Tennyson at Trinity and described him as 'a sort of Hyperion'. Their friendship dates from the time when they had all four left the University. I have a suspicion that Alfred Tennyson, dominated as he was by Arthur Hallam and his fellow apostles, did not take Frederick's odd friend too seriously and may even have treated him with patronising disdain. Since although Fitzgerald in his letters often refers to 'dear old Alfred', yet he also remarks that he was 'very droll and very wayward', and that 'he writes the names of his friends in water'. Twice every year throughout his life Fitzgerald would send an amicable letter to Farringford or Aldworth; but these letters were answered, not by the Laureate, but by Lady Tennyson or her son. It may have been the chill occasioned thereby to Fitzgerald's over-warm affections that induced him to underestimate the Laureate's later poems and to attribute to those of Frederick and Charles a comparative value which they did not in fact possess. To him, Alfred Tennyson was 'a man of genius who, I think, has crippled his growth by over-elaboration'. He frequently expressed the regret that Alfred had published anything after the 1842 volume. He condemned *The Princess* as 'a wretched waste of power' and contended that the songs in that poem (which we rightly regard as among the loveliest of all English lyrics) lacked 'the old champagne flavour'. He disliked *In Memoriam*. 'What can it do', he asked, 'but make us all sentimental?' 'I almost', he confessed, 'feel hopeless about Alfred now.'

Such errors of judgement should prepare us for Fitzgerald's curious overestimation of Frederick Tennyson's verse. He had a deep admiration for what he called Frederick's 'energetic, stirring, acquisitive and capacious soul'. He liked him for being 'strong, haughty and passionate'. His poetry appeared to be inspired by 'strong and genuine imagination'. It contained, so Fitzgerald asserted, 'heaps of single lines, couplets and stanzas which could consume all the Xs and Ys like stubble'. The only criticism he would permit himself was on the score of prolixity. 'A little', he wrote, 'of the vulgar faculty of popular tact is all that needs to be added to you.' 'Old Fred', he confessed many years later to Fanny Kemble, 'might have been one of the Three Brothers could he have compressed himself into something of the Sonnet compass; but he couldn't.' How far were these eulogies and these criticisms justified? Let me first examine the life and work of Frederick Tennyson.

4

Frederick Tennyson, the eldest surviving son of the Rev. George Tennyson, was born in June 1807 and died in 1898 in his ninety-first year. Unlike the other Tennysons, he possessed a fair complexion and blue eyes; his hair was scraped back from his forehead and fell in girlish ringlets down his back; there are those still living who can recall a huge domed forehead and this strange falling cluster of silver curls. At Eton, although good at cricket and Captain of the Oppidans, he was remembered mainly for his lack of social gifts. 'Rather a silent, solitary boy,' records Sir Francis Doyle, 'not always in perfect harmony with Keate.' This inability to adjust himself to his surroundings remained with him throughout his life. He described himself later as 'a person of gloomy insignificance and unsocial monomania'. He had a special loathing of what was then the aristocracy. He derided what he called 'the high jinks of the high nosed, who go about with well cut trousers and ill-arranged ideas'. Frederick's own clothes were Italian rather than well cut; nor can it be said that his ideas were ever well arranged.

He left Eton in 1827 and went first to his father's old college of St. John's and subsequently to Trinity, where he was later joined by Charles and Alfred. He obtained a Browne Medal for a Sapphic ode upon the Pyramids, but when he graduated in 1832 it was without distinction. It was originally intended that he should enter the Church, but this suggestion filled him with acute alarm. In 1833 he inherited a property near Grimsby and immediately left England for the Mediterranean. He remained absent for twenty-six years.

There is little of interest to record of Frederick Tennyson's long and self-imposed exile. For a time he lived in the island of Corfu, where a cousin was secretary to the High Commissioner. He thereafter migrated to Italy where he married Maria Giuliotti, daughter of the chief magistrate of Siena. We hear of him in 1841, playing a game of cricket at Naples with the officers of the *Bellerophon* and beating them by ninety runs. We hear of him later in Florence where he rented the Villa Gondi, and later the Villa Torrigiani. The main room in the latter residence had been decorated by Michael Angelo. Frederick was devoted to music and would sit for hours in this magnificent room while fiddlers played to him the compositions of Mozart. 'I am a regular family man', he wrote, 'with four children (the last of whom promises to be the most eccentric of a humorous set) and an umbrella.' And then in 1853, when he was forty-six years of age, an event occurred which altered the course of his life. He met the Brownings.

'Browning [he wrote] is a wonderful man with inexhaustible memory, animal spirits and bonhomie . . . Mrs. B. never goes out—being troubled like other inspired ladies with a chest—is a little unpretending woman, yet full of power, and, what is far better, loving-kindness; and never so happy as when she can get into the thick of mysterious Clairvoyants, Rappists, Ecstatics, and Swedenborgians.'

This meeting had two important results. Browning persuaded him to print his poetry. Mrs. Browning introduced him to spiritualism.

Frederick Tennyson's first volume was published in 1854 when he was forty-seven and was called *Days and Hours*. The choice of that title had evidently been suggested to him by the opening words of section 117 of *In Memoriam*. The book was not ill received. 'The poems', wrote Charles Kingsley, 'are the work of a finished scholar, of a man who knows all schools, who has profited more or less by all, and who can often express himself, while revelling in luxurious fancies, with a grace and terseness which Pope himself might have envied.' The word 'terseness' is the last word which I should myself apply to the poetry of Frederick Tennyson; other critics were less amiable than Charles Kingsley; and Frederick, being just as sensitive to adverse criticism as were his two brothers, remained silent thereafter for a space of thirty-six years.

In 1857 he left Italy and bought a house in Jersey overlooking St. Helier. He remained there for forty years. In 1880 his wife died; in 1890 at the age of eighty-three he published his second volume of poetry,

The Isles of Greece; in 1891 *Daphne* appeared; and in
1895 *Poems of the Day and Year*. He died in his son's
house in Kensington in February 1898. Such was the
uneventful and somewhat feckless life of Frederick
Tennyson.

Before I examine the nature of his poetic inspiration,
I must consider for a moment the effect upon his mind
and character of the Swedenborgian doctrines to which
he was introduced by Mrs. Browning. He had begun
with the more ordinary exercises in spiritualism, with
clairvoyants, with table-rapping and with automatic
writing. Before long, however, he found these manifestations insufficient; he indulged in wider experi-
ments. He became convinced that the spirits were
seeking to enter into direct personal communication
with him by means of electrical tickings in the air.
With desperate application he sought to interpret to
himself the meaning of these morse messages. He
was pleased and flattered when a medium disclosed
that he saw Frederick constantly and closely accompanied by the ghost of Mozart. He was convinced
that the millennium was approaching when there would
be no further barriers between the invisible and the
visible world. In 1872 he came into contact with a
certain Mr. Melville who assured him that he had
discovered a forgotten system for reading the stars
which would provide a new explanation of the masonic
signs and symbols. He accompanied Mr. Melville to
England and sought to convince the Grand Master of
the importance of this discovery. It was then that
Fitzgerald saw him for the last time. 'Quite grand',
he wrote to Fanny Kemble, 'and sincere in this as in
all else; with the Faith of a gigantic child, pathetic

and yet humorous to consider and consort with.' That
chance meeting with Mrs. Browning had produced a
permanent effect. 'The supernatural', wrote Frederick
Tennyson, 'has occupied and absorbed my whole soul
to the exclusion of almost every subject which the
Gorillas of this world most delight in, whether scientific, political or literary.' It has been said that in his
later years his faith in spiritualism suffered a decline.
Yet in 1887 when the Laureate visited him at St.
Helier he begged his famous brother to abandon
poetry for ever and to devote what years remained to
him of life to the study and propagation of the gospel
of Swedenborg. From all of which it may appear to
you that Frederick Tennyson, at least in the second
half of his life, was a most eccentric man. And what
about his poetry?

5

It is not my intention to weary you with the poems
which Frederick Tennyson published after he was
eighty years of age. *The Isles of Greece* is a long
rhythmical romance, written in clumsy blank verse,
the main feature of which is an imaginary love affair
between Sappho and Alcaeus. In this story Atthis is
made to appear as a child of two and Anaktoria as a
merchant princess. *Daphne and other Poems* is equally
long-winded, meaningless and ill composed. From
time to time one catches a faint echo of the Laureate's
mighty rhythm, but in fact, Frederick did not possess
a delicate ear for blank verse, even as he did not possess
much power of observation. It is a curious fact that
although he, unlike Alfred, had actually visited the
Greek islands, he is totally unable to convey the

Hellenic atmosphere. Alfred, who had never been to the Aegean, could write:

> 'For now the noonday quiet holds the hill:
> The grasshopper is silent in the grass;
> The lizard, with his shadow on the stone,
> Rests like a shadow, and the winds are dead.'

But Frederick who had spent almost a year in the Greek islands could introduce into a description of Mitylene the line 'Green plots alive with songs of happy birds'. Which suggests that he never noticed anything at all. Were these his only publications, then the name of Frederick Tennyson would not need to be recorded among our English poets. He would be of interest only as a pale reflection of his glorious brother, a reflection as pallid as the faint glow of a gibbous moon through the mist. His first volume, *Days and Hours*, does, however, deserve serious consideration, if only because it shows us how deep and lasting was the impress left upon the three brothers by the contrast between their own unhappy nerves and the protective assurances of Somersby.

There are, of course, certain passages in *Days and Hours* which are peculiar to Frederick himself. His colours are deeper and at times more violent than those used by either of his two brothers; the word 'purple' occurs with wearisome iteration; and the grapes and vine-leaves of Italy entwine themselves across almost every page. His natural irritability, which was more vivacious than either the neurasthenia of Charles or the black moods of Alfred, is often apparent. It echoes in a striking poem entitled *The First of March*:

'Larks twitter, martens glance, and curs from afar
Rage down the wind, and straight are heard no more;
Old wives creep out and scold and bang the door;
And clanging clocks grow angry in the air.'

We hear his 'unsocial monomania' in the couplet:

'And when the proud world, tyrannous and strong,
Tramples frail hearts into the dust of scorn.'

This sentiment is echoed in one of the few outstanding lines in *The Isles of Greece* when he rails at the elegant with the words:

'Your thoughts
Are harsh and boastful as the peacock's cry.'

And then, of course, we have the special diffuseness, the meaningless prolixity, which render most of Frederick's poems so wearisome to read. One's patience none the less is rewarded by sudden echoes of the authentic note of Somersby. We meet the Brook again, that simple little stream which fringed the rectory garden and by which all three of the Tennysons were so lastingly impressed. The flower beds, the pleached walk, even the lawn are mentioned. Strange, indeed, that twenty-six years later the memory of this ageing man should revert to the home which he had known in boyhood; that he should write of the church clock and of the benches under the porch; and that the sounds of Lincolnshire should come back to him so vividly among the violins and frescoes of his Florentine saloons:

'On the high wold, the last look of the sun
Burns like a beacon, over dale and stream;

> *The shouts have ceased, the laughter and the fun;*
> *The Grandma sleeps and peaceful be her dream;*
> *Only a hammer on an anvil rings;*
> *The day is dying—still the blackbird sings.'*

More interesting even than these sudden nostalgic glimpses is that sense of spiritual loneliness, of twilight fear, which haunts many of the finest poems which his great brother wrote. Frederick also could hear these 'prophetic voices low'; he also was attuned to:

> *'Dim thoughts, that reach us from the Infinite*
> *Faint as far seas, or twilight in eclipse;'*

he also could:

> *'see from off Time's dim gray shore*
> *The sunken tide of the world's blessed years.'*

He also could feel himself abandoned upon a moonless plain, and he also could be stirred almost to major poetry by the mystery of the half-light which comes before the dawn:

> *'Just then, 'tween Day and Night,*
> *I heard a wild bird singing in the dawn*
> *Far over hill, and stream, and wood and lawn*
> *That solitary magic took its flight,*
> *That holy, tender utterance of delight,*
> *By loving echoes deep into the forest drawn.'*

6

In the second section of this lecture I described how the three Tennyson boys composed their earliest poems together in the intensive domesticity of their attic bedroom. In the fifth section I have tried to show how Frederick Tennyson, living all those years in Italy and sundered from his two brothers in mind and spirit, was only able to rise above the middle levels of his talents when visited by memories of Somersby, or when haunted by that twilight fear which flickers like some marsh-light above the swamps of Tennysonian gloom. In the concluding sections I shall consider the life and work of the second of the three brothers, Charles.

If there be any purpose in this triple confrontation it is to enable you for a short space to view one of the greatest of our English poets from an unaccustomed angle. Here you have three brothers, inheriting a similar neurotic disposition, bred and educated in almost identical circumstances, sharing the same boyhood associations, and all endowed with a certain creative faculty. Each of these three brothers wrote poetry over a space of more than fifty years; to each of them the contrast between the security of Somersby and the harsh clangour of the outside world remained a recurrent source of inspiration; but whereas Frederick wrote a few pretty stanzas, and whereas Charles composed a number of admirable sonnets, Alfred had the power to cause these simple rectory tunes to wail and thunder and resound . . . which indicates that genius is not a matter of environment but derives from the fortuitous combination of certain hidden cells.

There is little to record of the placid life of Charles Tennyson. He was a year older than Alfred and shared with him the miseries of Louth grammar school, the domestic education of Somersby, and the rigours of their father's irritable temperament. The two brothers matriculated at Trinity on the same day

in February 1828. Charles won a Bell scholarship, graduated in 1832, and three years later became vicar of Grasby, a small hamlet in his native Lincolnshire. In 1836 he married Louisa Sellwood, whose younger sister became in later years the Laureate's devoted and admiring wife. In 1837 he inherited a property from his great-uncle Samuel Turner of Caistor and assumed the additional surname of Turner; it was as Charles Tennyson-Turner that he was thereafter known. He devoted his whole life to the needs of his small and backward parish; he rebuilt the vicarage and restored the church and the school; he was without children and interested himself in the composition of sonnets, the study of Italian, and the minute observation of nature. He died in April 1879, at the age of seventy.

In spite of this placid and seemingly unruffled existence, Charles had full share of the family neurosis and eccentricity. Shortly after his marriage he suffered a complete nervous breakdown and for a space of time he had to be segregated from all contact with the outer world. His appearance was strange indeed; his swarthy face was framed in long untidy ringlets; although as unkempt as the rest of the Tennysons, he took particular trouble about his clothes; the cuffs of his shirt were turned back over his coat sleeves in the manner of Count d'Orsay; he shared with Septimus, Alfred and Arthur, a liking for enormous black capes and large sombreros. His voice was gruff and deep; it was in his intonation, and in that of his sister Emily, that the Lincolnshire accent was most noticeable. When confronted with strangers he would actually tremble with fear. After a short period of estrangement in the early years of their marriage, his wife, who would refer to him as 'Cubbie', watched over him with a selfless devotion. Three weeks after his death she followed him to the grave.

Although the Laureate did not possess or preserve any deep family affections, there is no doubt that Charles was closer to him than any other of his brothers and sisters. When staggering under the shock of Arthur Hallam's death, Alfred had written section nine of *In Memoriam* which contains the following wounding stanza:

> *'My Arthur, whom I shall not see*
> *Till all my widow'd race be run;*
> *Dear as the mother to the son,*
> *More than my brothers are to me.'*

It may have been this stanza which, when *In Memoriam* was first published anonymously, induced a reviewer to remark that 'these verses have evidently been composed by the widow of a military man'. In any case the stanza caused offence to Charles Tennyson-Turner. One would have supposed that, on learning this, Alfred would have excluded the offending passage from the published edition. He did nothing of the sort. He merely added section seventy-nine; and we are glad that he did so, since it provides us with a valuable statement of the contrasting appeal of Somersby and Arthur Hallam:

> *' "More than my brothers are to me,"—*
> *Let this not vex thee, noble heart!*
> *I know thee of what force thou art*
> *To hold the costliest love in fee.*

But thou and I are one in kind,
 As moulded like in Nature's mint;
 And hill and wood and field did print
The same sweet forms in either mind.

For us the same cold streamlet curl'd
 Thro' all its eddying coves; the same
 All winds that roam the twilight came
In whispers of the beauteous world.

At one dear knee we proferr'd vows
 One lesson from one book we learn'd,
 Ere childhood's flaxen ringlet turn'd
To black and brown on kindred brows.

And so my wealth resembles thine,
 But he was rich where I was poor,
 And he supplied my want the more
As his unlikeness fitted mine.'

When many years afterwards the news of Charles's death reached Farringford the Laureate composed a commemorative poem entitled *Midnight, June 30 1879.* It is not a successful ode, since the poet's attention was distracted from his grief at the death of a beloved brother, by his fury at the vagaries of the British climate. There is far too much about the 'cuckoo of a joyless June' being succeeded by 'the cuckoo of a worse July'. But it does contain two stanzas which are worth quotation:

'And thro' this midnight breaks the sun
 Of sixty years away,
The light of days when life begun,
The days that seem to-day.

When all my griefs were shared with thee,
   As all my hopes were thine—
As all thou wert was one with me,
   May all thou art be mine!'

7

The intimate association between Charles and Alfred during their early youth is signalised by the fact that they each produced their first independent volume of poetry in the same year. In March 1830 Charles published in Cambridge a volume entitled *Sonnets and Fugitive Pieces*. In June 1830 Alfred published with Effingham Wilson in London *Poems, Chiefly Lyrical*, thereafter to be known as the '1830 volume'. The two books were sent by the kindly Arthur Hallam with a covering note to Leigh Hunt, who was then editing *The Tatler*. Hallam forestalled Leigh Hunt's probable criticism by suggesting that the poems by the two Tennyson brothers might not appeal to the common reader but 'only to the elect church of Urania, which we know to be small and in tribulation'. Leigh Hunt responded immediately. He devoted four successive reviews in *The Tatler* to an examination of Charles's sonnets and Alfred's lyrics. 'We have had great pleasure', he wrote, 'in stating that we have seen no such poetical writing since the last volume of Mr. Keats; and that the authors, who are both young men, we believe at College, may take their stand at once among the first poets of the day.' It is interesting to record that at the time Leigh Hunt believed that Charles showed the greater promise of the two. He was, however, too experienced a critic not to detect a certain absence of energy in Charles's compositions,

'I was fearful', he wrote later, 'of what he would come to, by certain misgivings in his poetry and a want of active poetic faith.'

Even more curious was the impression made by Charles's first volume of sonnets upon Wordsworth, who was visiting Cambridge at the time. 'We have', he wrote in November 1830, 'a respectable show of blossom in poetry—two brothers of the name of Tennyson, one in particular not a little promising.' We might have assumed from this remark that Wordsworth had noticed that Alfred possessed genius, whereas Charles was gifted only with a delicate talent. But it was not so. When Emerson visited Rydal Mount in 1848 Wordsworth remarked to him 'that he had thought an elder brother of Tennyson at first the better poet, but must now reckon Alfred the true one'.

Coleridge also was much impressed by Charles's first volume. 'The old man at Highgate', wrote Arthur Hallam to Emily Tennyson, 'has rejoiced over him.' This rejoicing, however, was not entirely un-critical. There exists in the British Museum a copy of this 1830 edition of Charles's sonnets with annotations in Coleridge's hand. It is true that he dubbed the sonnet *To a Lark* as 'one of the finest in the language'; it is true that he scribbled the more general comment that Charles Tennyson 'stood between Wordsworth and Southey partaking of the excellencies of both'. But he was too acute not to observe the absence of any compelling poetic force. 'The feeling', he annotates at one moment, 'seems to me fluttering and unsteady, pouncing and skimming on a succession of truisms.'

The Laureate himself would always maintain in later years that Charles's sonnets had 'all the tenderness of the Greek epigram'. 'I sometimes think', he said to Canon Rawnsley, 'that of their kind, there is nothing equal to them in English poetry.' 'I at least', he said again, 'rank my brother's sonnets next to those of the three Olympians'—Shakespeare, Milton and Wordsworth. This view was shared by Sir Henry Taylor. 'There are none', he wrote, 'in the language more beautiful in their sincerity and truth.' Only the Brownings maintained the startling opinion that Frederick Tennyson was a greater poet.

How much of this contemporary adulation can be accepted to-day? A more modern critic has, in my opinion, struck a happier balance. 'The sonnets of Charles Tennyson-Turner', he writes, 'live because their freshness conquers an almost unparalleled technical casualness.' It is on this more moderate note that I propose to examine in conclusion the poetry of Charles Tennyson.

8

After publication in 1830 of his first volume of poetry, Charles Tennyson was afflicted with one of those prolonged silences which were apt to descend on all the Tennysons. For thirty-four years he remained dumb and it was not till 1864 that he again ventured into print. The collection of sonnets published in that year was followed by two further collections in 1868 and 1873; after his death the whole of his work was issued under the title *Collected Sonnets, Old and New*, with a biographical memoir by his nephew Hallam Tennyson and a critical appreciation by James Spedding.

It may have been that his prolonged silence was occasioned by ill-health or that he felt himself over-shadowed by his illustrious younger brother. Charles Tennyson-Turner was more than a diffident man; he was almost morbidly modest. He became obsessed with the conviction that he possessed no original talent whatsoever and that his sonnets were no more than imitations and recollections of the work of others. Even robust writers can be afflicted with this obses-sion; it is a price paid for extreme and oversensitive intellectual integrity. Leslie Stephen, to whose memory this lecture is dedicated, was one of the most healthy minded of all our men of letters; yet even he could be assailed by doubts regarding his own authenticity. 'I always suffer', he wrote to Croom Robertson, 'from a latent conviction that I am an impostor and that somebody will find me out.' Charles Tennyson was no more of an impostor than was Leslie Stephen; yet with him diffidence developed almost into a disease. He never realised that he was a true poet, whose talents, although restricted, were original, delicate, sincere, and above all refreshingly spontaneous. And his life was clouded by long dark periods when he became convinced that such inspiration as he possessed had deserted him for ever:

> 'The edge of thought was blunted by the stress
> Of the hard world; my fancy had wax'd dull,
> All nature seem'd less nobly beautiful—
> Robbed of her grandeur and her loveliness;
> Methought the Muse within my heart had died.'

Nor did he ever believe, as Frederick sometimes believed, that his Muse, even when present to him,

could compete with his great brother's mightier res-
onance:

> *'But still I may misuse some honest theme,*
> *Tinkling this idle outgrowth of my brain;*
> *A hair amid the harpstrings! My weak words*
> *May pass unheard among the rolling chords.'*

The modesty of Charles's pretension—so different
from Frederick's ambitious diffuseness—served him
well. He would have failed miserably had he attempted
to write on the grand scale; where he succeeded was
in the delicate restricted and sensitive rendering of
small observed incidents. The sonnet entitled *Letty's
Globe* is familiar to us from the anthologies; it is not
—to my mind—the best of Charles's poems. He
possessed an original and charming capacity for identifying himself with tiny things. 'O Thou' he wrote:

> *'Oh Thou, who givest to the woodland wren*
> *A throat, like to a little light-set door*
> *That opens to his early joy . . .'*

His sympathies were instantaneous; let me read to
you a sonnet which he wrote when on holiday in
Wales on seeing the cattle trucks pass down the line
from Holyhead to London.

> *'My open window overlooked the rails,*
> *When suddenly, a cattle train went by,*
> *Rapt, in a moment from my pitying eye,*
> *As from their lowing mates in Irish vales;*
> *Close-pack'd and mute they stood, as close as bees,*
> *Bewildered with their fright and narrow room;*
> *'Twas sad to see that meek-eyed hecatomb,*
> *So fiercely hurried past our summer seas,*
> *Our happy bathers and our fresh sea-breeze,*
> *And hills of blooming heather, to their doom.'*

This gift of rapid sympathy extends even to inanimate objects; Charles enjoyed writing tender sonnets upon such things as abandoned rocking-horses, buoy-bells, a canary's empty cage, scarecrows and even hydraulic rams. Delicate was his touch, even fragile, as light and quick as 'the morning beam along the gossamer'. His sonnets suffer, however, from a curious clumsiness of diction; neither he nor Frederick possessed their brother's amazing sensitiveness to sounds. The following sonnet, entitled *The Lattice at Sunrise*, conveys the charm as well as the ungainliness of Charles's manner:

> '*As on my bed at dawn I mus'd and pray'd,*
> *I saw my lattice prankt upon the wall,*
> *The flaunting leaves and flitting birds withal—*
> *A sunny phantom interlaced with shade;*
> *"Thanks be to heaven", in happy mood I said,*
> *"What sweeter aid my matins could befall*
> *Than this fair glory from the East hath made?*
> *What holy sleights hath God, the Lord of all,*
> *To bid us feel and see! we are not free*
> *To say we see not, for the glory comes*
> *Nightly and daily, like the flowing sea;*
> *His lustre pierceth through the midnight glooms*
> *And, at prime hour, behold! He follows me*
> *With golden shadows to my secret rooms!"* '

One cannot imagine Alfred Tennyson permitting himself those ugly internal assonances of 'see' and 'free' and 'feel'. And yet the poem does contain something of Charles's fleeting sunbeam delicacy.

I have begun by indicating those aspects of Charles Tennyson's poetic talent which differentiated him from his elder and his younger brother. I must conclude on a more Tennysonian note. We have Somersby again, with its familiar domestic atmosphere, coming with that tug at the heart which assailed all the Tennysons when they recalled their boyhood years. 'And from the grove', writes Charles Tennyson:

> '*And from the grove which skirts this garden glade*
> *I had my earliest thoughts of love and spring.*'

And finally, we have that curious flickering loneliness which one finds in the better poems of Frederick, and which suggested again and again to Alfred some of his most immortal lines. For underneath the sentimental gentleness of Charles's poetry, detached from the delicate radiance of the world he loved, there brooded what he called 'the dark twilight of an autumn dawn'. It is this almost mystic sense of loneliness which echoes in the lines which Coleridge so much admired:

> '*Disordered music, deep and tear-compelling,*
> *Like siren voices pealing o'er the seas.*'

It is this which colours the fine sonnet called *A Forest Lake* with its concluding chords:

> '*Or when cool eve is busy on thy shores,*
> *With trails of purple shadow from the West,*
> *Or dusking in the wake of tardy oars.*'

And it is this which inspired the haunting lines:

> '*I'd bid that crumbled mound from Babylon*
> *Come looming up at sundown, with the moan*
> *Of evening winds . . .*'

It would indeed be foolish to contend that either of Alfred Tennyson's two brothers can rank among our major poets. Frederick was too wild, too eccentric, too diffuse: Charles too limited and too evanescent. But each of them serves to throw some light upon the complicated temperament of their younger brother; and to help us better to understand the jangled nerves, the brooding melancholy, the spiritual loneliness of that sensitive mystic; and the grandeur of the poetry that he wrote.

IV

SWINBURNE AND BAUDELAIRE

IV

SWINBURNE AND BAUDELAIRE

MORE than five years ago I read to the Royal Society of Literature a paper in which I tried to trace the relations between Swinburne and Baudelaire and to account for the curious circumstance that the author of the *Fleurs du Mal* should have produced upon the receptive English poet an influence transitory only, and in fact superficial. I endeavoured to construct from this confrontation of one poet with another a whole theory of Swinburne's powers of acceptance; I came to the conclusion that his receptive faculties had ossified in his early twenties: and I indicated that had Swinburne flamed hysterically to the influence of Baudelaire even as he caught fire from Victor Hugo or the Elizabethans, we should have had many more *Poems and Ballads* but we should not have had *Atalanta*.

When I had finished my paper, the late Sir Edmund Gosse, who as you know was the greatest living authority on Swinburne, took me aside. 'You were', he said, '*very nearly* right about Swinburne. But you were not *wholly* right. I advise you to think over the subject carefully, and then to revise your essay. You will find it worth while.'

Since that May afternoon in 1925 much material has come to light. The main trend of my thesis remains, I think, unaltered. But I am all too glad to profit by this opportunity to revise some of my conclusions, to expand some of my data, and to give what I hope is a saner and more considered interpretation.

In general the treatment of a poet's work in terms of comparison with the work of some other poet is, as a procedure of criticism, arid and jejune. Poetry is an act of secret experience, and to interpret that experience in the light of its more overt manifestations is in almost every case to mistake the accidental for the veritable.

The making of books about books is an undertaking both pleasurable and even remunerative: but too much research may lead one away from the central high-road, and all excursions into the wide meadows of plagiarism 'influences' and analogies are but wanderings from the path. A poet is a poet because he is himself: he may remind us of other poets: he may have drawn from other poets a persistent inclination to respond to certain sides of experience rather than to certain other sides of experience: the key to which he sets his song may have been set even by the tuning fork of some quite minor contemporary: but the song itself is his. Let it be stated at the outset that the comparative method is not in every case a fruitful, although it may seem a scholarly, method of approach.

It may be contended, however—and this present study must stand or fall by this contention—that there are certain poets whose mental and physical apparatus are so closely analogous, the circumstances of whose childhood and adolescent impressions are so strikingly similar, that a confrontation between them may, if reasonably handled, illumine aspects of their temperament which, unless viewed from this side angle, might remain shrouded. Two such poets are Baudelaire and Swinburne. By stating their similarities; by analysing their disparities; by indicating the wide divergence of their development; by recognising initially that they were so alike, and by examining thereafter why they were so unlike, one can, perhaps, attain to a fresh aspect of this familiar vista, and observe facets in both of them which may not, either from the front or even from the back, have been apparent before.

Let us begin with the similarities. They are striking enough. Swinburne and Baudelaire could both in after life look back upon a childhood of sunrise happiness. True it is that the intense happiness of Baudelaire's childhood was marred by the death of his father when the poet was six years old and clouded in the following year when his mother married General Aupick. True it is also that there is little apparent similarity between the boudoir atmosphere of Baudelaire's childhood and the ponies and bathing of Northumberland and the Isle of Wight. The open-air normality of Swinburne's childhood is not reflected in the stuffy luxury of Baudelaire's passionate devotion to his mother, in the rebellious jealousy which his step-father's presence and discipline subsequently induced. But for both of them there existed that nursery background with its strong appeal to the protective yearnings of their joint infantilism.

A second curious element in their early biographies was a strong eighteenth-century atmosphere to which they were both fortuitously exposed. Baudelaire's father who, before the Revolution, had been connected with the French patricians, always retained an exaggerated pre-Revolution manner. Swinburne's grandfather, up at Capheaton, had known Voltaire and had been the friend of Mirabeau. He inculcated into his little red-haired grandson the rigid distinction of the old régime. In both of them this chance influence developed an extreme regard for external conduct. With Baudelaire, as we know, it was evolved into the ideal of the 'Dandy'—an anglicanism which it is difficult for English people to understand. Externally it led to the affectations of his manner—his pink gloves, his absurd clothes, his parrot, and his silken muffler. Less externally it betrayed itself by his tight jerky movements, his delicate, almost creeping walk, the apparently effeminate precision of his every gesture. And more importantly it induced a patrician habit of mind, a habit rendered more intensive by his embittered reaction against all that General Aupick stood for— against the violent authority of the barrack square. And in its ultimate expression it accounts for the theory of 'Art for Art's sake'—the theory, ascetic rather than aesthetic, that the artist should exist only for his art.

The effect on Swinburne of old Sir John at Capheaton was, if less intense, then equally recognisable. The elaborate courtesy of Swinburne, those continental bowings, that disconcerting kissing of the female hand, the poker rigidity of his later years, can all be traced back to Capheaton, to those walks among the endless laurel shrubberies, when his grandfather would explain to him that the most fervent Jacobin should not abandon the elegancies of external conduct.

Thereafter the school careers of both of them were

marred by failure. Baudelaire was actually expelled from Louis le Grand. Swinburne, at Eton, was less unfortunate. His tutor merely suggested to Admiral Swinburne that Algernon might do better somewhere else. They both began their school days with exemplary docility and ended them in an atmosphere of rebellion and disgrace.

The adventures of their adolescence were equally analogous. Swinburne at Balliol rejected the prescribed curriculum and went off upon the tangents of scholarship: Baudelaire as a student specialised in dog-latin and plunged into those gulfs of indolence which were to become the obsession and the menace of his later years. They both succumbed to the temptations of inebriation—Swinburne to brandy, Baudelaire to drugs. They both refused thereafter to work for the professions prescribed for them by their parents. Baudelaire was destined by his stepfather for diplomacy: the Admiral decreed that it would be nice for Algernon to enter one of the Inns of Court. Each of these two poets preferred to devote his talents to literature and to live a bachelor existence upon his own resources. Baudelaire, no less than Swinburne, began by writing articles for the press, and it is significant that in each case their attention was first drawn to art criticism, and that their earlier articles dealt with contemporary exhibitions of pictures. Each of them again received a strong impulse, not from the literature of his own country, but from a foreign author who became the object of his idolatry. Victor Hugo was no less important to Swinburne than was Edgar Allan Poe to Baudelaire. They both began composing verses at about the same period of their development and they both postponed the publication of these verses for several years. And finally, to complete this sum of coincidences, they were both on publication faced with a prosecution for obscenity. The *Fleurs du Mal* as published by M. Poulet Malassis were actually condemned: Mr. Moxon only escaped prosecution by the skin of his teeth.

Such analogies, it must be admitted, are mainly accidental. Similar coincidences occur in the careers of many poets. The strange similarity between the development of Baudelaire and that of Swinburne can, however, be pressed farther. For starting from this identical background of an elegant childhood; passing through the analogous phases of an interrupted school career, a turbulent period at the University; rejecting, as they both rejected, the professions open to them, preferring to cling rather to the penurious and the independent; yet they both retained during the period of their life in London or in Paris an atmosphere of aloofness from the very circles which they delighted to frequent. Baudelaire, in his attic rooms at the Hotel Pimodan, in the garret existence to which with his declining fortune he thereafter degenerated, always remained the gentleman of family who had visited Bohemia by condescension. True it was that he would accompany Nadar and the rest to the lowest resorts of the city, that he would sit there in the cafés of the quarter drinking sleepily while the others caroused. But he remained for ever withdrawn from any direct participation in their more orgiac pleasures, and the hour would come when Baudelaire, with his shirt cuffs shining spotless above the sleeves of his great riding coat, would trip off along the Rue Vaugirard—'Walking', as Nadar described it, 'as if on eggs.'

A similar detachment characterised Swinburne's conduct at Tudor House. George Meredith, who was sensitive to social distinctions, was irritated by the patrician airs which Swinburne, quite unconsciously, adopted. Rossetti himself was more tolerant, though even Rossetti at moments wished that Swinburne would consent to be a trifle more untidy, would consent after all to enjoy his own adolescence. Both Swinburne and Baudelaire appeared irritatingly unreal to their friends.

Nor was it only in their attitude to their own selected companions that the two poets manifest a strange identity. They both reacted similarly to the atmosphere of their age. It is not perhaps far fetched to contend that mid-Victorianism, that curious social phenomenon which the French characterise by the word 'Philpopard', descended upon Paris some fifteen years before it obscured the Hanoverian gaiety of London. It is at least accurate to state that the *bourgeois* conventionalism against which Baudelaire reacted so vehemently in the later 'forties under Louis Philippe, was in essence identical with that great middle-class fog which descended upon England in the 'sixties. And against this pervading atmosphere of negation, against this oppressive blanket of precaution, both poets revolted in a precisely similar manner. Externally they desired to shock. Internally they endeavoured to retreat into the ivory tower of 'Art for Art's sake', or if you prefer the French word, of 'Dandyisme'. You are probably familiar with the many stories of Baudelaire's calculated indiscretions. He would sit silent at a café in the presence of some stranger who had joined their company. Suddenly he would lean towards him. 'Do you not find', he would inquire, 'that the brains of new-born babies have a slight after-taste of nuts?' Swinburne's own conduct in uncongenial company was exactly analogous. He shocked Lord Tennyson profoundly by declaiming in his high falsetto the most unbecoming of after-dinner monologues. It was with the greatest difficulty that Lord Houghton was able to put it right. And to what motive other than a determined desire to horrify the *bourgeois* can one attribute such gestures of revolt as the Cannibal Club, his own shrill conversations with Sir Richard Burton, or his proceedings at Étretat? I do not contend that all that de Maupassant has written of the villa which Swinburne shared with Powell bears any relation to the actual facts. But clearly Swinburne's desire to shock de Maupassant is on a par with Baudelaire's constant wish to horrify Vavasseur, Nadar, and the rest.

For in fact to neither of them did these extravagances come naturally. Swinburne had a sense of deportment which was almost laughable. Baudelaire had a touch of distinction which was more real to him than all his Satanic affectations. Yet both were impelled by reaction against pervading propriety to indulge in these schoolboy acts of impishness, which conflict strangely both with the adult dignity of Baudelaire and with the eternal child dignity of Swinburne.

Behind all these eccentricities of conduct remains the basic analogy between these two men, that fundamental affliction which prevented either of them from developing on normal lines. Nothing is more obnoxious than to dwell unnecessarily upon the sexual adjustments of a great poet. It may be argued with some justification, however, that the poetic development of these two men cannot properly be understood unless reference is at some point made to their physical abnormalities. They were neither of them perverted in the accepted meaning of the term. But for both of them the sexual impulse was deformed by partial impotence forcing them to derive from cerebral excitation that relief which they were physically denied.

Both of them experienced two love affairs, and in each case the first was unhappy and the second grotesque. Swinburne fell in love, or thought that he fell in love, with a Miss Simon. She laughed at him and wrung from him perhaps the finest of all his lyrics—the *Triumph of Time*. Baudelaire's affair with Madame Sabatier was even more pathetic. It is difficult to be quite certain about Madame Sabatier. The Goncourts refer to her as 'une vivandière de faunes'—'a barmaid for satyrs'. And yet she figures in the memories of others as a gay and charming lady, as 'La Présidente' of an exclusive literary circle, as a woman of considerable physical and mental charm. Baudelaire in any case fell in love with her. He addressed to her during two years anonymous letters inspired by the most ardent passion. Finally he confessed that he was himself the author of this correspondence. She was delighted and, much to Baudelaire's embarrassment, offered to recompense his loyalty and devotion. He mumbled excuses. There was Monsieur Mosselmann who paid the rent of Madame Sabatier's flat and might object to her having a lover. Madame Sabatier waved aside these scruples. And thus Baudelaire was forced in the last resort to confess his own physical inadequacy. The letter in which he did so still exists. It is a pathetic document.

As a counterpart to the unhappy affairs with Miss Simon and Madame Sabatier you have the grotesque connections with Adah Isaacs Menken and Jeanne Duval. Mrs. Menken was a circus rider of a certain age who wrote, and even published, the most sentimental verse. It was Rossetti who pushed Swinburne into this absurd connection with Mrs. Menken. He took him to the Aquarium to observe the lady in the part of Mazeppa. There was no response. He then informed each of them that the other was passionately in love. The incidents which followed are too grotesque to bear narration. The connection between Baudelaire and Jeanne Duval, the mulatto, though far more poignant and more durable, was equally sterile. It is important thus to realise that the love affairs of both these poets were a source of acid disappointment, humiliation, and shame. And to a certain point, but only to a certain point, they both reacted to it in a similar manner.

It is not necessary to enter into any detailed examination of the analogies which exist between *Poems and Ballads* and the *Fleurs du Mal*. These analogies are sufficiently apparent. You have in both an embittered reticence, an acid savour of frustration. In both you have a sad insistence upon 'the expense of spirit in a waste of shame'. Baudelaire no less than Swinburne, in his pathetic endeavour to extract something positive from all these cruel negatives, crushes out from the barren leaves of disappointment the bruised poisons of pain. And in both you have again the ideal of the statuesque in woman—the porphyry giantess of Baudelaire; the 'fair and fearful' Atalanta.

Such points are obvious: should any of you consider

1863 that the review was received. Further communications, including some of the foolish erotic poems that Swinburne thereafter composed, were addressed to Baudelaire through Whistler and his friend Fantin-Latour. It was not, however, until October 10, 1863, that Baudelaire replied. This letter, which was welcoming and courteous, was entrusted to Nadar, who was about to travel to London. At the last moment Nadar was tempted to take a balloon trip to Brussels. The letter was forgotten: many years afterwards it was discovered in a drawer. It has always been supposed that this abortive correspondence represented the only communications which passed between Baudelaire and Swinburne and it has even been contended that the latter's subsequent repudiation of the French poet was due to his taking offence at never having received Baudelaire's reply. M. Lafourcade in his excellent book *La Jeunesse de Swinburne* has disproved this legend.   He has discovered letters of Swinburne's which refer to an 'exchange of messages and courtesies' between Baudelaire and himself. The fact remains, however, that the two poets, although Swinburne was frequently in Paris, never met.

In April of 1866 a false report of Baudelaire's death reached London. Swinburne at once wrote to a friend in Paris asking for more information regarding 'the death of a man whom I deeply admired and believed in'. Before receiving a reply he composed the *Ave atque Vale*, that magnificent pagan requiem with which you are all familiar. A few days later the news was received that the earlier rumour was in fact false. Baudelaire, it is true, had a stroke at Namur and was lying in a nursing home deprived of the powers of consecutive speech. Swinburne was much distressed by this premature obituary and was with difficulty prevented from destroying the manuscript of the *Ave atque Vale*. Baudelaire lingered on, aphasiac and wretched, till August of 1867. Swinburne's memorial verses were included in the second series of *Poems and Ballads* published in 1878. That is all that is known of the external relations between Baudelaire and Swinburne.

Yet there exists an epilogue. Swinburne was twenty-five when he wrote the *Spectator* review. He was under thirty when he composed the *Ave atque Vale*. When he was sixty-four he objected to the inclusion of that poem in the Anthology of 1901. 'I never', he wrote, 'had really much in common with Baudelaire.' How are we to explain this apostasy? Not by the fact that Baudelaire had not responded very readily to his own overtures. Not by the fact that Baudelaire had been disrespectful to Victor Hugo—the idol of Swinburne's boyhood and adult enthusiasms. Not even by the fact that Watts-Dunton, who was acutely jealous of every pre-Putney influence, imposed upon Swinburne the repudiation of all former heroes. But essentially by the fact that it was true. 'I never had really much in common with Baudelaire.' No statement could be more accurate. No statement, perhaps, could be more damaging to Swinburne's renown. For although, as has been shown, they were temperamentally akin, yet they differed widely in the quality of their intelligence. Baudelaire, for all his sardonic reticence, was profound. Swinburne, for all his ebullient brilliance, was superficial. No wonder that, in the days when he had ceased to be a poet, the memory of Baudelaire became for

Swinburne a painful centre of self-criticism and self-reproach.

Let me, before I analyse the causes of this divergence, return for a moment to that first careless rapture of the Spring of 1862, to Swinburne's first excited confrontation with the *Fleurs du Mal*. 'He has chosen', thus wrote the young English poet flaming exotically in a Paris Turkish bath, 'he has chosen to dwell upon sad and strange things,—the perverse happiness and wayward sorrows of exceptional people. . . . Not the luxuries of pleasure in their simplest first form, but the sharp and cruel enjoyments of pain, the acid relish of suffering felt or inflicted.' Such, at the moment, was the immediate effect on Swinburne of the *Fleurs du Mal*, and you will agree that no more accurate description could be found for that side of Swinburne's own talent which had already by then expressed itself in such poems as *Félise*, *Dolores*, and *Faustine*. Let us recollect also that of all the English poets, Swinburne was the most sensitive to purely literary inspiration. The great, the formative experiences of his life had always been, were always to remain, literary experiences: the world of reality was for him but an evanescent shadow. His emotions were stirred only by what he read in books.

It may therefore appear strange that a man who had responded with such flaming violence to the Elizabethans, to Hugo, to Landor, and even to Mr. Charles Wells, should have recognised in a French poet an inspiration so identical with his own, and should have responded thereto with an enthusiasm which, although intense for the moment, was but transitory. When studying this point five years ago I imagined that I had found an explanation which, although seemingly fantastic, was yet tenable. I came, as I have said, to the conclusion that Swinburne's receptive faculties became rigid and ossified shortly after his twenty-first year. It is possible indeed to argue that all the inspirations which guided Swinburne throughout his long life had, with the possible exception of his Putney baby-worship (and even that might be ascribed to the Victor-Hugo inspiration), all been absorbed and experienced before the end of his first year at Balliol. None of his subsequent experiences had any lasting effect upon the temper of his mind. He might, for instance, have been profoundly influenced by the pre-Raphaelites had he met them some two years previously; naturally he was influenced by the pre-Raphaelites, but it is possible to show that their effect upon him was less intense and far less durable than the effect, let us say, of Walter Savage Landor. Similarly, it might be contended, that had Swinburne experienced the *Fleurs du Mal* in 1856 instead of in 1862, his enthusiasm for Baudelaire would have transcended his undiscriminating and in fact school-boyish passion for Victor Hugo. There is something in this contention. In fact it may be questioned whether it is possible to understand Swinburne, or to account for the endless repetitions of his themes, unless we take it as an axiom that his receptivity declined at an abnormally early age. And yet I now feel that his retreat from Baudelaire must be ascribed to causes even more recondite; and it is these causes which illumine that strange circumstance that Swinburne, on ceasing to be a heresy, failed to be a doctrine, whereas the influence of Baudelaire even to-day is solemn, penetrating, and profound.

In analysing the ebullient superficiality of Swinburne, in examining the reticent profundity of Baudelaire, it is easy to lose oneself in a mass of words. I should wish, at the outset of the concluding section of this lecture, to reduce to its simplest terms of expression the essential divergence between them. I should state it baldly as follows: Baudelaire was a man of supreme intelligence; Swinburne was not a man of supreme intelligence.

This statement requires, of course, some defence. I should frame my defence under the following headings.

It would be far beyond the scope of this paper to embark at this stage upon any definition of what is meant by intelligence. Let us confine ourselves to one of its most constant and recognisable symptoms. Let us confine ourselves to the great gift of curiosity. No one, I think, can study Swinburne without being appalled by the narrow range of his interests. His intense volubility misleads one at moments by the appearance of mental energy. To put it in another way, his verbal energy is so overpowering that we are all too apt to mistake it for an energy of mind; his scholarship again is so vehement, so enthusiastic, that we forget at moments that he possessed no insight—nay, no desire even for insight—into the devouring fact. You are all familiar with that curious narcotised lethargy which comes over one when one reads Swinburne. The attention, as one reads, ceases to be a concentrated attention—the eye passes onwards, the ear is pleasurably stimulated by the cadences, but the mind is not engaged. For Swinburne is an event only in the emotions; he is scarcely ever an event in the mind.

It is not fair perhaps to judge a poet by the importance of his attitude towards external affairs. I can well imagine that Baudelaire's own response, let us say, to foreign politics, would, had he ever indulged in such excursions, have been as childish as Swinburne's hysteria on the subject of Napoleon III or his senile jollification over the Boer War. That is not the point, for poetry is an internal, not an external thing. The point is that Swinburne was not even interested in himself. He was so un-self-conscious that for large stretches of time he became actually unconscious. There are wide gaps and periods of anaesthesia in Swinburne's life. He was not of those 'pour qui le monde sensible existe'. And thus, whereas Swinburne had much that was beautiful to sing, he had very little that was even averagely interesting to say.

Baudelaire, on the other hand, was intensely, almost morbidly, preoccupied by his own personality. 'La sensibilité', he wrote, 'de chacun: C'est son génie.' Baudelaire throughout his life was passionately inquisitive. 'J'ai cultivé', he wrote 'mon hystérie avec jouissance et terreur'—such an exploitation of his own neurosis would have been impossible to Swinburne. Baudelaire possessed an almost cynical curiosity for the more unusual symptoms of human psychology. Swinburne manifested a childish indifference to the characters of other people. I remember Sir Edmund Gosse telling me once that Swinburne had no real conception of what his particular cronies, such as Howell, Powell, and Simeon Solomon were really like. Gosse at one moment endeavoured to enlighten him. Swinburne refused to believe him. 'No English gentleman', he answered, 'would *do* such things.' Only a man as impervious to reality as Swinburne would have dreamt of foisting Anglican deportment upon such men as Solomon and

Howell. It is in such trivial stories that one recaptures the essential fatuity of Swinburne's habits of thought.

True it is that Swinburne, especially in later life, was an immensely industrious man. Far be it from me to suggest that intensive scholarship is sometimes an escape from indolence of mind. And yet when one considers what months of labour, what forces of enthusiasm, Swinburne devoted to the most minor Elizabethan,—when one realises what optimism inspired and sustained his defence of the prophetic books of Blake—one can scarcely resist the impression that he sought in these exacting studies a safe anchorage for talents which he felt instinctively were volatile, impulsive, and diffuse.

Contrast with this the embittered indolence of Baudelaire. 'I must acquire', he wrote, 'the habit of industry—the day will come when it will be all that remains to me.' 'Travailler', he wrote again, 'est moins ennuyeux que s'amuser'—and yet no poet has paid so warm a tribute to the privilege of idleness, to that 'loisir' which he felt had been the nursery of his genius. He describes himself somewhere as 'le type de paresseux nerveux'—the nervous sluggard. It would be a mistake to attribute his lack of concentration to laudanum alone. It was a deliberate conviction that he need not start to work until he had ceased to think. This was by no means an otiose excuse for his own indolence. Far more was it a symptom of his subordination of all his faculties to the creative faculty alone.

For whereas Baudelaire drew his experience directly from life, Swinburne's experiences, meagre as they were, are in addition second-hand. 'J'ai plus de souvenirs', wrote Baudelaire in one of the most famous of his poems, 'que si j'avais mille ans.' Swinburne's memories in contrast furnish a pitiable little group of childhood recollections—a storm upon the Ostend steamer, the streams in April among the Northumberland hills, the sea-gulls at Freshwater. External impressions only, and even as such impressions of no deep significance. Whereas the sombre memory of Baudelaire was crowded with gaunt visions of solitary hours when he had sat there alone in contemplation of himself.

Many of you will have read Mr. Peter Quennell's brilliant and finely written essays on the Symbolist movement. His study of Baudelaire contains a passage which expresses exactly what I am endeavouring to convey. 'Here', he writes, 'a man had been born quite incapable of normal satisfactions, of the normal facile small pains and smaller compensatory pleasures: had he willed it even, he would have proved himself lacking in the bastard ingenuity which has enabled countless smaller writers to soften the acerbities of life with the borrowed amenities of art.' It was in this way that Baudelaire, as Mr. Quennell says, reached 'a footing of almost complete subordination to his art'.

This subordination was of a rigidly stoic nature. The very reticence of Baudelaire stands in grim contrast to Swinburne's incapacity for even average economy of words. There is no single poem of Swinburne's which would not benefit by omissions: the poems of Baudelaire are rigidly curtailed. It is this scrupulous limitation of his talent which gives to the work of Baudelaire its durability: it is the reckless diffusion of his talent which robs the work of Swinburne of the importance which it ought to possess.

Allow me in conclusion to resume the tangled thread

of this discourse. I have endeavoured to indicate the curious similarities, the startling coincidences of up-bringing, temperament, and environment which linked these two poets in their life and in their work. I have given instances of how, in many ways, they both of them responded to these influences in a precisely similar manner. I have implied that Swinburne's sub-sequent retreat from Baudelaire was due partly to his arrested development, partly to the pain occasioned by too great an identity of temperament, and partly to the fact that ultimately and essentially Swinburne was not preoccupied by the problems which became the whole centre of Baudelaire's thoughts. And as an explanation of this final gap between them I have indicated the divergent qualities of their intelligence—the powerful brooding intelligence of Baudelaire, the volatile and superficial fantasy of Swinburne. They were both faced by an almost identic psycho-sexual problem. Swinburne escaped from it by surrendering himself to the hysteria of hero-worship and the narcotics of extensive study. Baudelaire never escaped from it.

And thus it came that whereas the mind of Baude-laire collapsed finally under the weight of his accum-ulated memories, the mind of Swinburne escaped into diurnal familiarity with superficial painless things. At a stage of their respective developments when Swin-burne was writing ditties about the perambulators on Putney Heath, Baudelaire was writing that lapidary line which must for ever constitute his epitaph:

Ne cherchez plus mon cœur: les bêtes l'ont mangé.

With that solemn cadence in your ears I leave you to consider which of these two men was the greater poet.

V

THE PRACTICE OF BIOGRAPHY

V

THE PRACTICE OF BIOGRAPHY

In an age when, within a few hours, men can be transported from Croydon to Khartoum; when children, seated in their own small chairs, can watch Presidents being inaugurated, atomic bombs exploding, or fish with round eyes and muslin fins circling in an aquarium; when experience has transcended imagination and reality has proved more terrible than any phantom; —in such an age it is inevitable that the sense of wonder should become atrophied, that the fictional should lose its stimulus, and that people should prefer to read about what happened in the unfrightening past rather than about what may happen in our awful present or future.

The modern propensity to write and read biographies is not, however, due solely to a desire to escape from anxiety. The young men and maidens who, without possessing any compulsive creative gift, think that it would be nice to write a book, are attracted to this form of composition, since it provides them with a ready-made plot, need entail no tremendous energy of research, and enables them to relieve their sensibility without placing too taut a strain upon their imagination. The common reader, for his part, feels that in learning about the adventures, passions and misfortunes of real heroes and heroines he is indulging in no idle relaxation, but is acquiring knowledge, is 'teaching himself history'. That, when all is said and done, is a commendable thing to feel. For him modern fiction has become so intricate, so self-centred and so cruel that it leaves behind it an after-tone of bewilderment and distress: it is both more comforting and more instructive to read about the past. In this manner biographies accumulate and prosper.

It is noticeable also that in ages of faith, when the minds of men are fixed upon the eternal verities and the life after death, the practice of biography tends to decline; whereas in the succeeding periods of doubt, speculation and scepticism, the interest in human behaviour increases. Thus in the fourteenth century in England we had all the elements of good biography, whereas in the succeeding century the interest waned: in the sixteenth century again the impulse of curiosity became active and productive, only to recede with the advent of puritanism in the age that followed. Then came the eighteenth century and the phase of enlightened humanism which produced our greatest biographies, whereas with the revival of theological preoccupations in the Victorian epoch both the demand and the supply declined. The twentieth century should have coincided with a powerful revival of pure biography, but although many books are published, it does not appear that any modern formula has as yet become established.

The ease with which biographies are written and sold to-day entails a danger that an art so perfectly attuned to the Anglo-Saxon temperament may become inflated. Moreover, the tendency manifested by many elderly ladies and gentlemen to publish autobiographies—hoping thereby to recapture the security of their childhood and to demonstrate the triumph of character over environment—will still further debase this currency. It may therefore be opportune to reconsider whether there do in fact exist any fundamental biographical principles; and to examine what are the perils and illnesses to which the art of biography is by its very nature exposed.

The Oxford English Dictionary defines Biography as 'the history of the lives of individual men, as a branch of literature'. This excellent definition contains within itself the three principles that any serious biographer should observe. A biography must be 'history', in the sense that it must be accurate and depict a person in relation to his times. It must describe an 'individual', with all the gradations of human character, and not merely present a type of virtue or of vice. And it must be composed as 'a branch of literature', in that it must be written in grammatical English and with an adequate feeling for style.

A biography combining all these three principles can be classed as a 'pure' biography: a biography that violates any one of these principles, or combines them in incorrect proportions, must be classed as an 'impure' biography. A pure biography is written with no purpose other than that of conveying to the reader an authentic portrait of the individual whose life is being narrated. A biography is rendered impure when some extraneous purpose intrudes to distort the accuracy of presentation.

Thus Voltaire's *Histoire de Charles XII*, although written and composed with consummate mastery, is not a 'pure' biography, in that it does not depict an individual character in relation to the background of the times. Carlyle's *Life of John Sterling*, although from the literary point of view his most attractive work, is 'impure' biography, since it is not very precise, not a true portrait, and written with a purpose other than that of the direct delineation of an individual. Walton's *Lives* are without question masterpieces of English prose; but they sin against the principles of biography, since Walton is not describing human beings, but types of the particular form of quietism that he himself regards as desirable. Many biographies, on the other hand, are perfectly historical, really do paint, even if with clumsy strokes, the portrait of an individual, but are so badly written that they cannot for one instant qualify as literature. A biography therefore which does not combine all three of these fundamental principles must be defined as impure.

The development of the art throughout the ages shows us how ancient and how recurrent are these 'extraneous purposes' by which the purity of biography is infected. There is no better method of isolating the principles of pure biography than to trace the sources of these infections.

2

The original cause of all biography was the desire to commemorate the illustrious dead. A leader dies: his tribe or family feel that some strength has passed from them: they seek to perpetuate his magic by a monument. Cairns and monoliths arise; we have the regal sites of mighty pyramids; men scale the precipices and engrave a cenotaph upon the rocks of Bisitun; epics and sagas sing the legends of tribal heroes; the wrath of Achilles is rendered immortal and to this day men read with elation of the endurance and resource of Ithacan Odysseus; Balder and Beowulf come to swell the paean; the whole world echoes with the praise of famous men. With this epic strain there mingle elegies and laments. Widow-biographies are an early phenomenon; to the *Complaint of Deor* we add *The Wife's Complaint*. This commemorative instinct is bad for pure biography, since it leads the commemorator to concentrate solely upon the strength and virtue of his hero and to omit all weakness or shadow. Endemic, and sometimes epidemic, is this passion for commemoration; it has infected biography throughout the centuries.

The impulse is not primitive only; it operates to this day. It is but natural that when a great man dies his family should desire that his life should be written in such a manner as to emphasise his nobility and to hide his faults. Even the most enlightened survivors are inclined to entrust the biography of their dead chief, not to an outsider who may take too objective a view of his subject, but to some inexpert, but loyal, member of the family, who can be trusted to suppress all unfavourable truth. Occasionally the widow herself undertakes the task, sometimes with results as fantastic as those of Lady Burton's biography of her erratic but gifted husband. Even when an honest outsider is commissioned, he may be precluded from outspokenness by a laudable desire not to wound the susceptibilities of those to whom he is obliged. An even more curious and subtle effect of such family-inspired biographies is that the author may become influenced by the petty grievances or animosities cherished by the hero or his widow in their later years; instead of creating an impression of greatness he creates an impression of smallness. A classic instance of this unintentional diminution of a hero's character is provided by General Sir C. Callwell's *Life and Letters of Sir Henry Wilson*: there have been others since. The commemorative instinct assuredly operates in devious ways; but it is always perilous to pure biography.

A second extraneous purpose is the didactic purpose. People have always been tempted to take the lives of individual men as examples of virtue, or as cautionary tales indicative of the ill-effects of self-indulgence or ambition. Plutarch himself, the father of biography, admitted that he chose his characters as types of certain virtues and vices and as examples for emulation or avoidance by the young. Yet Plutarch happened to be a natural biographer, in that he was passionately interested in the way that individuals behaved; thus, although his lives of Anthony or Alcibiades, for instance, were intended to be cautionary tales, he soon forgot his didactic purpose in the fascination exercised upon his mind by the splendour of Anthony or the gaiety of Alcibiades. Flashes of admiration and delight illumine his pages, until both he and his readers forget entirely that an extraneous purpose of moral precept ever existed.

It is not so with other hagiographers. The lives of

the saints and martyrs were not, it can be admitted, always intended to be historical accounts of individuals. Yet in more disguised form the didactic purpose continues to intrude upon biography; the desire to teach or preach, the desire to establish examples, the desire to illustrate some moral, theological, political, economic or social theory—all these irrelevant intentions infect biography with strong, and sometimes subtle, doses of impurity. The nineteenth-century biographers were most susceptible to the didactic temptation. 'The history of mankind', wrote Carlyle, 'is the history of its great men.' 'To find out these, clean the dirt from them, and to place them on their proper pedestal' appeared to him and his contemporaries a proper function of biography. This doctrine led to such impurities as *The Saintly Lives Series* in which, among other worthies, Lord Tennyson was portrayed, not as he was, but as the sort of Laureate that the author felt he ought to be. The reaction against the hagiography of the Victorians led to a development, valuable as a corrective, but, in its baser derivatives, damaging to the pure biographic stream. I refer to the introduction, by Froude and his successors and imitators, of the element of irony.

The satirical attitude of the biographer towards his subject may have come as a relief from the hagiography of the Victorians, but it can easily degenerate into false history and false psychology. Froude certainly provided a true picture of Mr. and Mrs. Carlyle; his portraits were condemned by his contemporaries as cynical, disloyal and in shocking bad taste. The influence of Samuel Butler came to transform Froude's attitude of negative scepticism into positive derision of conventional legends. Lytton Strachey, with his ironical titters, emerged as the deftest of iconoclasts; yet Strachey, who enjoyed paradox more than he respected precision, and who had little sense of history, exaggerated the lights and shadows of his portraits. His sketches were certainly vivid, personal and well written; but they were not 'history' in the sense that pure biography demands. In the hands of his imitators the manner of Strachey deteriorated so rapidly that it became an irritating habit of superciliousness. Philip Guedalla, with his trick of dramatic contrast, diminished the very real value of his writings by too great insistence on antithesis; his pictures became distorted and out of focus.

Irony is, in any case, a dangerous tincture and one that should be applied only with a sable brush; when daubed by vigorous arms it becomes wearisome and even offensive. It is not merely that the reader is irritated by a biographer who implies in chapter after chapter that he is himself more enlightened, sensitive, or sincere than the hero whom he is describing. It is also that biography, if taken seriously, is an exacting task and not one that can be carried through with a sneer. The drudgery of collecting and checking material, the mechanical labour of completing a long book, require an effort more continuous than can be sustained by glimpses of self-satisfaction. The biographer must be constantly fortified by a fundamental respect, or affection, for the person whom he is describing; if all that he experiences is superficial contempt, his work will turn to ashes and his energy wilt and fail. No writer can persist for five hundred pages in being funny at the expense of someone who is dead.

There are other poisons, other temptations, to which this difficult art is liable. Biography is always a collaboration between the author and his subject; always there must be the reflection of one temperament in the mirror of another. The biographer should thus be careful not to permit his own personality to intrude too markedly upon the personality that he is describing; he should be wary of assigning his own opinions, prejudices or affections to the man or woman whose life he writes; he should take special pains to deal fairly with views which he does not share, or interests that bore him; his egoism should be muzzled and kept on a chain. He should constantly remind himself that it is not an autobiography that he is composing, but the life of someone else; the statue of Modesty should dominate his study, a finger on her lips.

A further temptation that may afflict the affable biographer is that of adding to his narrative the colours of fiction or romance. He may seek to convey reality by introducing imaginary conversations, or to brighten his pages by inserting really beautiful passages of scenic description:

'As their little cavalcade breasted the hill and emerged from the grove of umbrella pines (*pineus pinea*) that crowned its summit, the fair city lay before them, basking all amethyst in the fading light. The Palazzo Pubblico had already melted into the pink and azure shadows of the Piazza del Campo, but the Torre del Mangia soared upwards, straight as a tulip against the sunset sky. Galeazzo turned to his venerable companion. "Messir", he said . . ." '

Such passages fail to convince the attentive reader, who is aware that umbrella pines are but few at Siena and that the company at the moment were travelling west to east. The imagination, as well as the self-assertiveness, of the author must be held in check.

Such then are the instincts, poisons and temptations that render biography impure. An undue desire to commemorate, a too earnest endeavour to teach or preach, a tendency to portray types rather than individuals, the temptation to enhance self-esteem by indulging in irony, the inability to describe selflessly, and the urge to slide into fiction or to indulge in fine writing;—all these are the pests and parasites that gnaw the leaves of purity. Yet these are negative precepts, indicating the faults that should be eschewed. Are there any positive principles that can be recommended to the intending biographer?

3

It is self-evident that he should not select a subject outside the range of his sympathy or the area of his general knowledge. It would thus be a mistake for a man to embark upon a life of Pope if he were ill-attuned to the heroic couplet and disliked small stratagems. It would be a mistake to start writing a life of Anselm without some knowledge of Plato's doctrine of ideas, or to embark upon Erasmus when ignorant of the humanities. It would be foolish for an Englishman to venture on a biography of Calvin Coolidge, without having spent at least a year at Amherst and absorbed the indelible quality of that academy.

The ideal subject is one of which the author has direct personal experience and with which he can enter into sympathetic relationship. This raises the question whether it is in fact possible for any author —however skilled, courageous, or sincere—to write a 'pure' biography of a contemporary. It is clear that it will be of great advantage to him to have been personally acquainted with his hero and to have seen him, not only in his moments of public triumph or efficiency, but also in those interludes of lassitude, dyspepsia, or elation that reveal the character of a man. Important it is also to be able to visualise a person, not in the set postures of official busts or portraits, but in the more illuminating attitudes of ordinary life. It is valuable to be able to recall the manner in which he coughed or grunted, the exact shape of his smile or frown, the sound of his laughter, and above all the tone of his voice. We are all conscious that the personality of our acquaintances is conveyed to us, not merely by their physical appearance and expression, but also by their accent and intonation. It is illuminating to be told that Bismarck spoke with the piping notes of a schoolboy, that Napoleon, when angry, relapsed into the Corsican manner of speech, or that Tennyson when reciting his poems used the broad vowels of the Lincolnshire wold. It is valuable also for a biographer to be personally acquainted with the men and women who exercised an influence upon the life of his subject and to be able, by his own judgement, to assess their relative value. 'How strange', he will reflect, 'that my hero could ever for one moment have been taken in by such a charlatan as I know X to have been!

How curious that he was never able to appreciate the shy wisdom, the fundamental integrity, of my dear friend Y!' This wider knowledge provides a system of triangulation, enabling the author to fix the position of his hero with greater accuracy than would ever be possible were he writing about people whom he had never personally known.

Such are the advantages—and they are immense—which the biographer enjoys when writing the life of a contemporary. The disadvantages are also apparent. He will be inhibited by his disinclination to offend the susceptibilities of survivors. It is not only that he will hesitate to wound the feelings of relations and friends; it is also that the enemies of his hero may still be living and will protest violently against any criticisms that may be made. To some extent he can evade this difficulty by refraining from expressing any personal opinion and relying solely upon the documents in the case. But the necessity of maintaining a certain level of taste, consideration, caution and kindliness, will certainly prevent him from revealing the truth in its most naked form.

Does this mean, I repeat, that it is impossible for an author to write a 'pure' biography of a contemporary? I do not think so. He will realise of course that, human nature being what it is, the reader of his book will pay more attention to those passages which reveal defects hitherto concealed, than to those which eulogise merits already familiar. The essential truth of any portrait depends upon the proper statement of relative values. A biographer should be aware that the 'startling revelation' is certain to startle, and will thus assume in the reader's mind and memory an importance out of proportion to the portrait as a whole. His revelations therefore should not be picked out in scarlet or orange but introduced in neutral tints. His aim should be, not to conceal defects or lamentable episodes, but to refer to them in such a manner as will indicate to the attentive reader that these shadows existed, without disconcerting the inattentive reader or wounding the legitimate feelings of surviving relations and friends. It is a question of tact and skill.

It has always interested me, when reading the biography of a person with whom I had been personally acquainted, to observe how the author deals with his faults. A device frequently adopted is to reveal the fault by denying its opposite. An extreme example of this method can be found in Sir Sidney Lee's biography of King Edward VII. Sir Sidney was an honest biographer, who desired to paint his portrait warts and all. I had often heard that King Edward was a voracious eater and that he was apt to pounce and gobble at the dishes placed before him. I wondered whether Sir Sidney would mention this genial characteristic and was impressed by the delicacy of his device. 'He had', wrote Sir Sidney, 'a splendid appetite at all times, and never toyed with his food.' It is by such ingenuity that the biographer is able to omit no detail and yet to cause no offence.

I should cite as an excellent example of the way in which an intelligent biographer can indicate defects without wounding feelings, Mr. Rupert Hart-Davis's biography of Sir Hugh Walpole. The attentive reader is made aware of all the lights and shadows in the character portrayed, whereas the inattentive reader is not for one moment startled or shocked. Every

weakness of Walpole's character is abundantly illustrated, yet the resultant impression is that of a gifted
and charming man. I recommend this work to all
those who question whether it is possible to write a
'pure' biography of a contemporary figure. The artist
has produced an authentic portrait owing to his sense
of values; without such a sense, any biography is
bound to be unconvincing.

4

It is here that a natural gift of selection is so valuable.
The aim is to convey the personality of some interesting individual to people or generations who never
knew him when alive. It is not possible for a biographer, even if he take twenty years and volumes, to
present the whole man to posterity. He can hope only,
by intelligent and honest selection, to convey the
impression of the aggregate of his hero's merits and
defects. If he allows himself to deck his portrait with
striking little snippets and tags, the unity of impression will be destroyed. His curiosity therefore
must be moderated by selection and taste; he must
preserve throughout a uniform tone; and he must try,
—he must try very hard,—to arrange his facts in the
right order.

'The value of every story', remarked Dr. Johnson,
'depends on its being true. A story is a picture, either
of an individual, or of life in general. If it be false, it
is a picture of nothing.' This precept should, I feel,
be inscribed in lapidary letters on the fly-leaf of every
biographer's note-book. A pure biography should
furnish its readers with information, encouragement
and comfort. It should provide, if I may again quote

Dr. Johnson, 'the parallel circumstances and kindred images to which we readily conform our minds'. It should remind the reader that great men and women also have passed through phases of doubt, discouragement and self-abasement; that—perhaps on the very eve of their noblest achievements—they have been assailed with diffidence, or have resigned themselves to the fact that their vitality is ebbing, their zest has gone, their memory has become unreliable, and their will-power decayed. Without seeking for one moment to preach a lesson, a good biography encourages people to believe that man's mind is in truth unconquerable and that character can triumph over the most hostile circumstances, provided only that it remains true to itself. Amusing books can be written about ridiculous people; fiction and romance can be twined as honeysuckle around the silliest head; but I am convinced that a pure biography, if its effect is to be more than momentary, can only be written about a person whom the writer and the reader can fundamentally respect.

Does this imply a return to hagiography? No, it implies only that the intending biographer should be as cautious in his choice of subject as in the method he pursues.

VI

ALEXANDER THE GREAT

VI

ALEXANDER THE GREAT

I

MULTIPLE and strange are the legends woven around the name of Alexander the Great. In the Moslem tradition he is represented as the young hero, horned as a ram, who cast down the idols of the heretics; the Persians assert that he was in fact the son of their own Darius; according to one early romance, he was the child of an Egyptian magician who taught them how to destroy armies by modelling them in wax and throwing their effigies upon a brazier. Even in our own earliest literature he figures as a fairy prince. 'The storie' begins the Monke in the *Canterbury Tales:*

> '*The storie of Alisaundre is so commune*
> *That every wight that hath discrecioun*
> *Hath heard somwhat or al of his fortune.*'

In spite of these romances, Alexander, although legendary, was never mythical. There are indeed few great figures of the past whose lives are so precisely documented; no less than five of his immediate friends wrote their memoirs. There was Ptolemy, one of the most effective of his younger generals, who founded the Egyptian dynasty which lasted for three hundred years and was extinguished only on that grim night when Cleopatra nursed the adder to her breast. There was the bluff Cretan sailor, Admiral Nearchus. There was Callisthenes, the nephew and pupil of Aristotle, who was appointed official historian and who came to a sorry end. There were Aristobulus and Onesicritus, both high-ranking officers in the army and navy. It was upon their first-hand and detailed records that Arrian and Plutarch based their biographies.

Yet even when the story has been stripped of all that is irrelevant or improbable, even when we have studied the facts accumulated and sifted by generations of scholars, there remains outside the radius of positive knowledge a haze of radiant and entrancing mystery; we are left with six enormous question marks.

Of what shape and substance was this miraculous youth? By what dreams and demons was his imagination haunted? What imperatives came to mould and steel his ambition? By what magnetic force was he able to keep his mixed army together in the wilds of Central Asia for almost eleven glorious but frightful years? What destiny impelled him to push onwards, ever further into the unknown? Above all what did Alexander really feel and think about himself?

This is not an account of campaigns, battles or conquests: it is an examination of the man himself. It is best therefore first to provide the reader with the stark outline of the story in almost diagrammatic form:

356 B.C.   Alexander is born at Pella, the son of Philip II, King of Macedonia and his wife Olympias, Princess of Epirus.

343 B.C.	He is instructed at Mieza by the philosopher Aristotle.
340 B.C.	In his father's absence he is appointed Regent of Macedonia and fights his first campaigns against the Balkan tribes.
338 B.C.	At the age of eighteen he commands the left wing of the Macedonian army at the battle of Chaeronea and defeats the combined forces of Thebes and Athens.
336 B.C.	On the assassination of his father he becomes King of Macedonia at the age of twenty.
335 B.C.	In lightning campaigns he reduces to submission the barbarians of the north, east and west, and after the capture and destruction of Thebes frightens the rest of Greece into electing him their Commander-in-Chief.
334 B.C.	At the age of twenty-two he leads his army into Asia and wins the battle of the Granicus.
333 B.C.	He defeats the King of Persia at the battle of Issus.
333-331 B.C.	He consolidates his conquests in Asia Minor and is recognised as Pharaoh of Egypt. He captures Tyre and thereby deprives Persia of all sea power.
331 B.C.	At the battle of Gaugamela he finally defeats Darius and becomes King of Kings.
330 B.C.	The capture and death of Darius.
329-328 B.C.	He pushes on into Central Asia.
327-326 B.C.	The expedition into India.

325 B.C.   The return from India.
324 B.C.   Planning for further conquest.
June 13, 323 B.C. He dies at Babylon aged thirty-two
                  years and eight months.

The mere skeleton of the story, as written down in
dates, distances and sequences, is sufficiently astonishing. At the age of twenty-five this ardent stripling
had conquered the whole known world. The facts
are familiar: it is the psychological background that
remains perplexing.

2

Even around the circumstances of his conception
and birth there hung, during his own lifetime, a cloud
of mystery and superstition.

His father, Philip II, was a man of outstanding
military and diplomatic genius. It was all very well for
Demosthenes to denounce him in the Athenian agora
as 'a barbarous pest from Macedonia—that country
which cannot even provide a decent slave'. Within a
few years from his accession Philip had disciplined his
rough peasants and mountaineers into a standing army,
possessed of the invincible phalanx, which the mer-
cenary forces of the Greek city-states were wholly
unable to withstand. The victory of Chaeronea in 338
rendered Philip the master of all Greece. He was
assassinated at Edessa at the very summit of his cap-
acities in the year 336.

It is recounted that Philip first met Olympias,
mother of Alexander, at a spring festival on the island
of Samothrace. Theirs was not a happy marriage.
Olympias, who claimed descent from Achilles, came
from the rugged mountains of Epirus and was half

Albanian. A Medea-like figure, she indulged in Orphic mysteries and Dionysiac orgies, and was regarded by the citizens of Pella as an awe-inspiring witch, who cast spells upon her enemies and roasted her rivals over slow charcoal fires.

On the night before her marriage Olympias dreamt that a thunderbolt, enveloped in flames, had crashed into her womb; she took much pleasure in repeating this story to her attendants. A few nights later, Philip, on retiring to rest, looked through the keyhole of his wife's bedroom. He was surprised to see her in bed with an enormous snake. He sent a mission to Delphi to ascertain the meaning of this portent. The oracle replied that the snake must have been some god in disguise; that as a punishment for his irreverence Philip would lose (as indeed happened) the sight of the eye that he had applied to the keyhole; and that he must immediately sacrifice to Zeus Ammon, the god of the Oasis of Siwa in Egypt, and for ever thereafter hold this god in special reverence.

Parts of this fairy story must have been repeated to Alexander by his nursery maids when he was a child. He did not dismiss it as entirely fantastic. Philip also remained forever uncertain whether Alexander was really his human son. From that moment he kept aloof from Olympias in superstitious fear. He had other wives and other children, all of whom were roasted alive by Olympias after his death. And she herself was eventually murdered seven years after her great son had been buried among the sands of Egypt.

In spite of the dark doubts that would assail him, in spite of the disgraceful scenes that would occur between them, Philip from the first recognised the amazing physical and intellectual power of his heir. He took him as a child away from the women and placed him in charge of his kinsman Leonidas, with instructions that the boy should be nurtured with the utmost rigour. He was conditioned to endure without a whimper the extremes of heat and cold, of thirst and hunger; he was never allowed either a blanket for his limbs or a pillow on which to rest his golden head. It was this training that endowed his tough little body with almost superhuman powers of endurance. Yet for all his muscular energy, for all his incredible audacity, Alexander never quite conformed to the type of perfectly normal male. He was bored by games: he hated having to preside so frequently at athletic contests: and women left him cold. Indeed, so distressed was Olympias at the sexual frigidity of her son, that she summoned from Thessaly the courtesan Kalixeina and told her to initiate Alexander into the precocious passions expected of a Macedonian prince. Kalixeina was not a success.

When Alexander was thirteen years of age, his father summoned to Macedonia the philosopher Aristotle, the greatest teacher of all time. In order to remove him from the fierce petting of Olympias and the court atmosphere of Pella and Edessa, Philip told Aristotle to set up his school in the remote country village of Mieza. Alexander was accompanied to this school by certain picked sons of the Macedonian nobility, among whom were Hephaestion, Ptolemy and Harpalus, the closest companions of his later adventures. The boys were taught ethics, politics, rhetoric and science; they were instructed to avoid the asperities of the Macedonian dialect and to speak in the pure Attic mode; and they were told that the purpose of education was to acquire, not information only, but an abiding zest for further knowledge. Unflagging curiosity, Aristotle insisted, was the sure test of the intelligent man.

Much of Alexander's delightful inquisitiveness must be ascribed to the teaching of Aristotle. During all his campaigns he never lost his passionate interest in geography, anthropology, meteorology and botany. He took an amateur interest in medicine and would embarrass his generals by insisting on prescribing for them potions and poultices of his own invention. For this favoured and important pupil Aristotle wrote two special treatises on the art of ruling and the method of establishing colonies. He set before him the ideal of a philosopher king, ruling the world for the benefit of all mankind; he inspired him with the wholly un-Greek conception of the brotherhood and equality of man; he suggested to him the surmise of a divinely appointed mission. In later years Alexander referred to certain 'esoteric mysteries' which Aristotle had also communicated to him and begged his former master not to impart them to others. Undoubtedly Aristotle stimulated the natural mysticism of his pupil, training him to believe in the transcendental, never to admit the impossible, and to dream dreams such as Hephaestion alone of his companions could even begin to understand. Certainly it was from Aristotle that he derived an obstinate faith in his own destiny, a certain fatalism, and those vast visions that haunted him until his death.

3

Such parentage and training were not what a modern psychiatrist would recommend. For his father, Alexander felt admiration, mingled with resentment and even hatred. To his demon mother he was profoundly devoted. In after years, when he was far away in Sogdiana, letters reached him from Antipater, whom he had left behind as Regent of Macedonia, complaining that Olympias was rendering ordinary government, and even life, impossible. 'Antipater does not understand', sighed Alexander, 'that three hundred letters from him mean less to me than one tear from my mother's eyes.' Yet as a child he had often seen her slobbering in rage, or writhing upon the floor in maenad delirium. And as a boy, on the wild night that followed the victory of Chaeronea, he had watched his father staggering intoxicated over the naked corpses of Athenians, brandishing his sword like any drunken Scythian, and belching out the jingle, '*Demosthenes, Demosthenous,*' under the great grey mountains and the watching moon. Leonidas had conditioned his body: Aristotle his mind. These harsh experiences and tremendous influences were not such as to create an integrated personality. Alexander won many great victories by sheer force of will: but the greatest of all his victories was that which, with frequent set-backs, he achieved over the discordance within himself.

We know something at least about his personal appearance and habits. He was short of stature and muscularly built. He had long fair hair and was clean shaven. He had a tender skin, which burned scarlet and not brown in the sun of Asia. He had a way of leaning his head sideways, drooping it over his left shoulder. All authorities agree that he possessed, like Adolph Hitler, magnetic and 'astonishingly melting' eyes. He had a trick of suddenly looking upwards. To the charm and gentleness of his voice and bearing there are many testimonies. His rage, when it mastered him, could be terrific: strained by many battles and many wounds, he became irritable and impatient. He started to drink heavily. His power of work was phenomenal; he could do without sleep and food, yet from time to time, when exhaustion came upon him, he would retire to his tent and sleep without waking for thirty-six hours. Although in general modest and reticent, he would, when drunk, vaunt embarrassingly. All writers agree that a mysterious and delicious savour emanated from his person. Yet for all his charm and courtesy, he must have been a very formidable young man. Long after his death, Krateros, who was no neuropath, was walking slowly up the Sacred Way at Delphi. Turning a sharp corner, he came suddenly face to face with Lysippus' life-size statue of Alexander. The knees of Krateros began to knock together and the sweat beaded his forehead.

Such was the boy who at the age of twenty succeeded to the throne of Philip II and became possessed of the most powerful military weapon, the Macedonian phalanx, that the world had yet known. This famous formation consisted of 30,000 men, divided into six divisions of 5,000 each, and armed with the *sarissa*, or pike, twenty feet in length. Although the *sarissa* could outrange any contemporary weapon, and although the phalanx, with its shields locked and its pikes levelled, constituted an impenetrable human and would, if they so dared, treat himself. He, the descendant of Achilles, the pupil of Aristotle, was sneered at as a semi-barbarian, an untutored stripling, an uncouth colonial, who in his young pretension claimed membership, nay even leadership, of the pure-bred Hellenic family. Again and again do we find proofs of how strong within him was this desire to surmount this sense of cultural inferiority and to impose himself upon august Athens as an equal, a benefactor and a son. With what delight, after his first battle on the Granicus, must he have written with his own hand the proud declaration which accompanied the 300 Persian panoplies despatched to Athens: 'From Alexander and the Greeks (except the Spartans) these spoils of the barbarians who dwell in Asia.' Seven years later, when caught in an ambush in the Punjab and battling fiercely to cut his way out, he was heard to utter most revealing words. 'Oh Athens!', he shouted, 'if you only knew what perils I am undergoing in order to win glory in your eyes!' Surely such strange obsessions are more interesting than simple ambition.

It is true, as many historians have emphasised, that in forming his great army Philip had denuded the Macedonian exchequer and that if the State were not to go bankrupt, vast loot must immediately be secured. But Alexander never noticed money and was one of those impatient people who believe that finances always settle themselves. There was about him a super-natural recklessness which can only be explained by some belief in his divine mission, or at least some certainty that he was entitled to, and would receive, the special protection of the gods and heroes. In the early battles against the King of Persia, in the fierce

Multan. His attitude towards auguries was not wholly consistent. Sometimes, as at the Granicus, when his soothsayers said that the month was unpropitious for any grave hazard, he would force them to change the name of the month so that all would be well. At other times he would take such portents with great seriousness, as when he delayed the storming of Halicarnassus because a swallow had fluttered round his tent when he was enjoying his siesta. Again, when he was about to cross the Oxus, the entrails of the beasts he sacrificed proved in an ill-omened condition; he sought to persuade the hepatoscopist Aristander to deliver a more favourable interpretation; Aristander refused, and Alexander waited for days in a fever of impatience until the rams when cut open showed the sort of shape and colour of liver that would permit him to cross. He never took any risks with the foreign deities whom he encountered on his journeys. At Memphis he underwent all the ceremonies demanded of him by the Egyptian priesthood: at Babylon he sacrificed, with all the Chaldean ritual, to Bel.

Then we have the two perplexing stories of the Gordian knot and the visit to the oracle of Zeus Ammon at Siwa. In the temple at Gordium, near the modern Ankara, was preserved the waggon of Midas, the yoke of which was bound by a knot of cornel bark that seemed to have no end and no beginning. The prophecy was that he who could untie the knot would become master of Asia. The story put about by Alexander's subsequent detractors was that he cut the knot with his sword, exclaiming 'See, I have untied it'. Now all authorities are agreed that such an action was out of character, since Alexander was far too super-

stitious a man to cheat a prophecy. He certainly felt
that to fail utterly might diminish his reputation as a
miracle worker: what he probably did was to pull out
the pole pin, removing the yoke from the pole,
exclaiming as he did so, 'See, it is now loosened!'
But the interesting point about the story is that he
would certainly have regarded it as impious, or
hybristic, to cut the knot with his sword. He was not
that sort of man.

Even more mysterious was his pilgrimage to the
oasis of Siwa in Egypt to consult the oracle of Zeus
Ammon. From the delta of the Nile he marched west-
ward with but a few attendants as far as Mersa Matruh,
and then struck south. Within two days it had become
clear that the guides had utterly lost their bearings and
that the whole party would perish of thirst. At that
moment two serpents appeared, uttering words of
encouragement in the Greek language, and guided
them safely to where the palm trees of Siwa glimmered
beyond the sand. Alexander entered the holy of holies
alone; he emerged radiant with delight. He refused to
disclose what the oracle had revealed to him, beyond
saying that it had 'told him what he wished'. Had he
indeed been greeted as the son of the two-horned Zeus
of Africa, who had lain with Olympias in the guise of
a snake? Or had he been told only that he would
conquer the whole known world? Deliberately Alexander remained silent regarding the mystery of this
revelation. His men certainly half-believed that he
was the son of Ammon, and reviled him as such at the
time of the mutiny at Opis. And why, unless he wished
to give credence to the legend, was his head upon his
coinage flanked by two rams horns?

6

Of his military genius there can be no question whatsoever; it is wrong to assert that he merely inherited the great machine that Philip had created and that his enemies were weak. In every battle always he was outnumbered and he always triumphed by force of will. The speed of his movement was extraordinary and again and again we hear of him surprising the enemy by marching a hundred miles in three days and nights. He was astonishingly responsive to new conditions, and coped with equal dexterity with the tactics of the Tribulli and the Parthians, with the scythed chariots of Darius or the elephants of Porus. As a leader of men he was unsurpassed. He had an astonishing memory for names and faces and would before a battle ride through the ranks, calling each company, and even platoon, leader by his name. He would visit his men in hospital; see to their comforts and amusements; speak to them in their own rough dialect. Above all, he would never demand of them anything that he would not endure himself. Conspicuous in his shining helmet and great plume it was he always that led the assault; apart from many minor wounds he was severely wounded at least seven times, his wide ruddy torso, when he stripped it before them during the mutiny at Opis, was seen to be striped with scars. During the dreadful journey through the wastes of the Mekran he was offered some water in a helmet; although almost dead with thirst, he emptied the water on the ground. Yet even this does not wholly explain the will and magnetism that enabled him to keep those men together, marching they knew not the most fervent curiosity does not suffice to explain how the young man imagined that he could keep a Greek army together in the wilds of Asia and India after they had been sundered for ten years from their homes.

One explanation certainly is that Aristotle's views on geography were over-simplified. He taught his pupil that the earth was a flat and circular object like a plate, surrounded by the great rim of ocean. This theory induced many confusions in Alexander's mind. He imagined, for instance, that the Indus was in some manner connected with the Nile. Even more importantly he assumed that, once he had crossed the further river, known as the Ganges, he would reach the encircling Ocean and be able to transport his armies by sea, back through the Caspian and the Euxine, until, their masts decked with flowers, they sailed triumphantly into the harbour of Amphipolis or Therma, where only some thirty miles would separate them from their families and their homes. Thus to him it was a terrible disappointment when, on reaching the Punjab, his men refused to march any further. Only a few weeks, he believed, would have brought them to the encircling sea and an easy passage back to Macedonia. Their refusal meant that they would have to retrace the long and dangerous land journey that had taken him all those years. For three days he sulked, like Achilles, in his tent: he then gave way to the wishes of his army. It was a terrible return journey. Thirst and hunger assailed them in the wastes. But at last they reached Babylon. And then, as he was planning further explorations and enterprises, the fever seized upon his wounded wasted frame. As he lay dying, the army demanded to see him. The bearded veterans filed past his couch; he had the strength only to raise one hand in a final farewell.

I have seen the high mound of Babylon: I have heard the fountains of Pella and Edessa gurgle above the stony plain of Macedonia; I have watched the lizards dart across the carvings of Persepolis; I have stood in the snow-wind that rocks the poplars of Ecbatana. I have read most of the books that have been written around Alexander the Great. Yet, having visited the places that meant so much to him, having studied the records of his life, I am left with this sense of mystery. It is this entrancing sense that I have endeavoured to convey.

How came it that so sensible a man could perpetrate such senseless things? He may have hoped to fuse the Persians and the Greeks into a single master-race; he may have believed that his immense prestige and power would enable him to achieve Aristotle's ideal of the community, the *homonoia*, of mankind. But how for one instant—unless it was that some flash of Olympias' frenzy seized him—can he have ever supposed that a Greek would accept an Asiatic as an equal, or submit to the repulsive ceremony of the kow-tow? Great clemency was his, and much magnanimity; but at moments the Illyrian madness would capture him, and he would behave with barbaric ruthlessness, as when he so coldly murdered Parmenion, as when he tortured and humiliated Bessus, as when with his own hands he stabbed Kleitos, as when he ordered the brutal massacre of Massaga, as when in a passion he destroyed the city of Thebes.

A miracle he was, assuredly. I have preferred to present him to you as a mystery.

VII
NATURE IN GREEK POETRY

VII

NATURE IN GREEK POETRY

I

WHEN your Association asked me to be their President for 1951, I was flattered and alarmed. Flattered, since it is indeed a compliment to be asked to preside over your deliberations. Alarmed, since it may seem pretentious for one who has no claim to academic attainments to accept so honourable an invitation. I was thus relieved when Professor Richardson assured me that it was your custom from time to time to choose your Presidents from the ranks of the untutored. I have no wish, however, to appear before you, cowering in a protective cloud of self-depreciation. I am here simply as a person who has retained his delight in classical literature, and who is conscious that his present enjoyment of the classics would be less of a relaxation were it not for the constant assistance afforded him by Leaf and Loeb.

I have chosen for the theme of this address the ambitious title *Nature in Greek Poetry*. My excuse for venturing upon so hazardous a subject is that throughout my reading life I have devoted attention to the shifting forms of sensibility that have induced writers to notice and appraise differing aspects of external nature. Moreover, having travelled often, and lived sometimes, in the areas covered by Hellenic civilisation, I have been able to compare what the Greeks noticed with what I myself noticed, and thus to accumulate a store of contrasts and parallels, of strange identities and even stranger omissions.

I shall not of course be using the word 'Nature' in the sense of natural or physical philosophy or as relating to the many implications of the term φύσις. I shall be using it to signify the external world as seen by the poets, dramatists and philosophers whom I shall be considering. I shall be using it to include night and day, storm and sunshine, seas and mountains, landscape and scenery, animals and flowers. And I shall be asking why the Greeks, with their passionate devotion to beauty, remained comparatively indifferent to many areas of enjoyment, from which we, with our different sensibility, derive such constant solace or delight.

2

I shall begin with Homer, not because he provides in every respect a perfect example of what might be called the classical attitude towards nature, but because he was the great preceptor, whose images gave shape and colour to all later minds.

Clearly this is not the occasion to raise even the fringe of the Homeric controversy. For the purpose of this address I shall assume that the epics were written by an individual poet—possessing certain idiosyncrasies of experience and perception—who flourished in the island of Cos between 900 and 800 B.C. Indeed I doubt whether any person who approaches the epics from the purely literary point of view would deny that there runs through them a uniformity, or rather 'personality', of style, incompatible with the idea that they are no more than aggregations of previous or current lays and legends. In speaking of Homer, I shall thus take it for granted that I am describing the observations of an individual poet upon two contrasting types of scenery and climate, namely those of the Troad and those of the central Mediterranean and the Aegean.

Even the most superficial study of the Homeric poems should warn us against what Ruskin called the 'Pathetic Fallacy', namely our inclination to invent an atmosphere that was not there. We northerners, when we read the great Greek books, immediately become 'spell-bound among the clustering Cyclades'. To our imaginations such phrases as 'and the sun sank and darkness came on', or 'in the season of spring when the long days begin', or 'Chios that glistens more than any island of the sea', or 'when we reached Sunium the headland of Athens'—cease to be outright statements of fact and begin to shimmer with all manner of sentimental associations. We tend to assume that the dawns were always 'saffron-robed' or 'rosy-fingered', that the sea was always 'wine-dark' or 'violet', or 'purple', and that at night the great constellations wheeled majestically in a cloudless and unquenchable ether. We persuade ourselves that 'when the sun turns to the time of the loosening of the oxen' there will follow inevitably a flaming sunset; that in the ensuing darkness the planets will be scattered across a velvet sky; that the quiet dawn will come with a tinge of green and crocus and that thereafter will follow the bright morning, the 'divine daylight', the ἱερὸν ἦμαρ. Yet in the *Iliad* Homer was not describing a good climate; he was describing a bad climate. Those who have visited the Hellespont and have watched the windmills of Hissarlik whirling furiously in the northern gale, well know how much the climate of the Troad depends upon the direction of the wind. When the south wind, which men still call 'Notos', blows up from Africa, then indeed all is April and the apple-trees burst into bud. But when the north wind, which men still call 'Boreas', howls down from the Thracian uplands, then the whole world changes to a sullen chilly grey.

It is then that we realise that what Homer describes is not the eternal summer of our imagination, but the actual climate of the Troad, observed by a poet who knew and noted all its moods. A land of fog and sleet; a land of snow, scudding in blizzards, or falling silently from a black sky:

> 'As flakes of snow fall thick on a winter day, when Zeus the Counsellor has begun to snow, showering upon men his arrows. He lulls the winds and he snows continuously, till he has covered the summits of the high hills, and the uttermost headlands, and the grassy plains and the tillage of men; and the snow is spread over the harbours and the beaches of the grey sea; only the wave as it rolls in keeps away the snow.'

Surely this can be no stock passage culled from a traditional lay; it is something experienced, by the escarpment of Hissarlik; something noticed, seen.

Even in the *Odyssey*, with its warmer although scarcely more equable climate, the islands are not gilded by eternal sunshine, nor are the seas perpetually calm and blue. When Telemachus goes down to the shore to wash his limbs it is not some sparkling pool that he discovers; he finds only the 'grey sea water'.

increased. He then mentions six kinds of fruit trees and fourteen varieties of other trees. Nor was Homer in any sense a horticulturalist. His attitude towards flowers was allusive rather than intense. We do not find in any of his poems, or indeed in any Greek poems, the sympathetic botanical interest that led Virgil (who incidentally intended one day to write a long poem upon gardening) to describe the golden aster that grew by the Mella stream or the look of lupins in September. Homer does not tell us what flowers were to be found in the garden-beds of Alcinous, or of those that decked the meadows where the sirens sang. He does indeed tell us that in Calypso's island there were violets as well as the inevitable parsley or celery; he does observe how a field of corn blows in the wind, or the way the poppies droop their heads; he does mention the wild garlic and the as- phodels of the Elysian fields. Yet it is evident that he had no idea at all to what species the lotus belonged, and his general attitude towards botany was medicinal rather than aesthetic. It is true that in the *Hymn to Demeter* he mentions roses, crocuses and hyacinths, or bluebells, and that he describes a miraculous narcissus, bearing one hundred blossoms; it is true also that in the *Hymn to Apollo* he surprises us by noticing wild flowers in a wood—a most un-Hellenic movement of attention. Yet who am I to suggest that Homer was the author of the Homeric hymns?

In regard to animals, Homer was less unobservant. He tells how the cranes, when disturbed by man, rise and settle again a little distance off; he notices that dogs are apt to twitch and snuffle in their dreams; he has obviously some acquaintance with livestock; he observes exactly how a horse munches grass. Yet all these matters are viewed in relation to man and not independently. It is curious, for instance, that Homer shows no interest in fish; even the lovely dolphin of the Aegean is little more to him than a clumsy member of the countless tribes of the sea. Euripides was one of the few Greek writers who observed with pleasure the antics of a school of porpoises.

Homer's attitude towards Nature, as indeed that of most of the Greek poets, was thus general rather than particular, synthetic rather than analytical. He was interested in winds and weather, since they directly affected the occupations of man; but he was not in the least interested in minor beauties, since man as he passed could trample upon them or turn aside. Homer was only rarely a sentimentalist, but he did certainly possess and convey in his two epics certain sentiments which his successors either did not feel, or did not choose to express. Homer had a lively sense of earth's prevailing mood; he was conscious, as his successors were seldom conscious, of landscape and scenery, of spaces and distances. It was with a pleasure that we can recognise as almost an aesthetic pleasure, that he would describe how Iris floated down to earth lightly skimming over the peaks of the mountains. He was moved by the sight of promontories standing out suddenly in a flash of lightning; by the thought of sailors gladdened by the sight of a distant bonfire burning on the mountain side; by the great constellations as they turned. For him the seas and headlands, the dawns and sunsets, the long beaches and the small havens had an independent beauty. Such perception was only rarely equalled by the poets of the classical period.

Hesiod shared with Homer what seems to us, hardened as we are by the fierce vicissitudes of our own climate, an undue preoccupation with the state of the weather. He also was extremely sensitive to the north wind 'that blows across horse-breeding Thrace' and 'huddles the thick clouds'. Being an agriculturalist, he was naturally pessimistic: 'Full is the land of evils,' he complains, 'and full the sea.' Of the eight winds, Hesiod loathed four, and dismissed the other four as too variable to be praised. Much as he disliked the cold at Ascra, he disliked even more the summer heat 'when women are most wanton and men most weak'. At such seasons he longed for some clear spring under the shadow of a rock, where he could sleep through the noontide or 'drink bright wine'. Hesiod was not without moments of acute observation; he noticed, for instance, that the early shoots of a fig-tree have the shape 'of the foot-print that a crow makes'. But I doubt whether he ever really noticed the difference between grass and flowers, or admired the striped tulip of the Boeotian fields. Replete though his writings are with excellent advice and exhortation, they do not possess that sense of the symbolic solemnity of agricultural processes, of the emotional relationship between man and matter, that render the *Georgics* one of the finest nature poems in the world.

4

On leaving Homer and Hesiod for the great epochs that follow, I find myself faced with a problem of arrangement. If I take the poets and dramatists in their chronological sequence, noting how each in his turn had a different personal attitude towards natural beauty, I shall become entangled in all manner of reservations, repetitions and divergences. It is not their differences that are so significant, but their similarities. If, on the other hand, I select an arbitrary set of themes and consider to what extent, and for what reasons, these themes were treated differently at different periods, I shall be entangling my arguments with my illustrations and exposing you to wearisome bewilderment.

I propose therefore to separate my examples and illustrations from my main conclusions and to divide the former into two categories, taking first those beauties of nature to which the Greeks made little more than a perfunctory response, and secondly those which they observed with interest, reverence or pleasure. Under the first category would come sea, mountains, woods, scenery, flowers and animals. Under the second category would come spring, cold and heat, shade and water, night and stars, and light and air. Only when I have finished with my illustrations shall I try to deduce some general principles to explain why this most inquisitive, observant, and, in some ways sensitive, race, should have approached the beauties of nature, often with unawareness, often with indifference, often with anxiety or distaste.

We, with our strange Celtic admixture of thought and feeling, cannot even read the word 'Greece' upon a printed page without forming an immediate mental picture of blue seas and shining mountains. To the Greeks the sea was not a source of aesthetic emotion, but an essential and most perilous destiny. They regarded it with awe. How often do we find the sea associated, as in the famous chorus in the *Antigone*, with that most Greek of all epithets—the adjective δεινός, with its implications of religious solemnity and personal fear. The Greeks were conscious of the sea's majesty, even as they were conscious of its lustral or purifying qualities. 'The sea', writes Euripides in the *Iphigenia*, 'that washes away all human ills.' Yet to them it was never a placid or seductive element; it was grey and angry, roaring always, as in the *Clouds*, with a deep-sounding menace. It is not until we reach the second century that we find the poets referring to the sea in terms of anything but awe or apprehension. Moschus could speak of Europa and her companions, with baskets of roses in their hands, taking 'pleasure' in the sound of the waves. But it was not pleasure or any of the gentler emotions that the sea gave to the Greeks of the great century; for them it was an enemy and not a friend. How seldom, for instance, do we read in the post-Homeric poets of the delights of bathing; Callimachus' *Bath of Pallas* was a fresh-water affair, and even the nymphs of Alcaeus, when they wash their fair thighs, are careful to choose a section of the beach where a fresh-water river pours into the purple sea.

To us again it appears almost inconceivable that the Greeks should have derived no aesthetic pleasure from the beauty of their own mountains. At best they regarded them as the remote palaces of Olympian deities or as familiar home landmarks; at worst they were the haunts of malignant spirits and wild animals or the cause of extreme personal inconvenience. It may be true that Pindar, when using the epithet 'violet-crowned' for Athens, was thinking of the strange light that throbs in early autumn on Hymettus, but Aristophanes denounced that adjective as strained

and therefore ridiculous. How curious it is also that
the Athenians hardly mentioned the Lycabetus, which
to our minds is so dominant a feature of their immediate landscape. Aristophanes refers to it twice only, and
as a joking metaphor for 'a huge great chunk'. To
the Greeks, people who enjoyed mountains were either
mad or impelled by some wild Dionysian frenzy. The
only occasion, as Professor Hardie has noticed, when
mountains are referred to as 'lovely' is a passage in the
Critias; and then the epithet is applied to the unknown
and undiscovered mountains of a mythical Atlantis.

Forests and trees, moreover, either frightened or
bored the Greeks. They would never have understood
Juvenal's injunction that every poet should be *'cupidus
sylvarum'*. One only visited the forests when in search of
charcoal or when driven there by Dionysus, for the sole
purpose, it would seem, of pulling up pines. The olive
of course, Sophocles' 'grey-leaved olive that nurtures
our sons', was revered as an economic asset, as a sacred
speciality. But what mention is there of other trees?
We have Sappho's apple-tree, we have Theocritus'
reference to the wind in the pines, and we have Aristophanes' lovely line about the plane-tree whispering to
the elm. Not much assuredly; assuredly not much.

Scenery again, as we sentimentalists understand the
term, plays but a small part in the poetry of classical
Greece; the poets and the dramatists seem to have had
little conception of the beauty of space and distance;
they seldom noticed a view. The watchman in the
Agamemnon is not in the least entranced, as Macaulay
was entranced, by the thought of beacons answering
each other from peak to peak. We have the splendid
evocation of Prometheus:

'Oh bright ether, winged breezes, springs of rivers, and innumerable laughings of the sea! Oh mother-earth the universal! Oh all-seeing circle of the sun!—to you I call.'

But Prometheus was a fallen Titan and thus entitled to emit these impious invocations. We have that other famous cry of Philoctetes:

'Creeks and promontories, dens and lairs of mountain beasts, and mantling cliffs—'

yet in the very next line we are assured that this appeal is addressed to nature, only because there exists no god or man who can come to his assistance. The only passage that suggests an emotion comparable to that conveyed to us by wide prospects and distances is that in the first Chorus of the *Clouds*. But Aristophanes was, as I shall observe later, an exceptionally sensitive man; he noticed things that his contemporaries failed to notice.

It is not my impression that the Greeks took any lively or observant interest in flowers, except in so far as they were useful for cooking or symbols of the advent of spring. It is with suspicious vagueness that Pindar mentions the 'happy flowers of Aphrodite's garden' and we should remember that Pindar mistook the *anemone fulgens* for what he called 'a ruddy rose'. There is quite a pretty flower-passage in the *Hippolytus* and both Euripides and Aristophanes speak with approbation of the smilax. But what in fact was the Greek smilax? Was it holm-oak, or yew, or bind-weed, or only the kidney bean? The Greeks were no aesthetic botanists, although Aristotle, or one of his pupils, does consider in the *Problemata* why some roses smell more strongly than others. Nor did they care for gardens, other than kitchen gardens.

Plato in the *Laws* dismisses the art of gardening as 'a not ungraceful childishness'. The garden mentioned in the *Acharnians* was no more than a vegetable garden, its borders edged with parsley and rue. We can contrast Xenophon's account of his country house near Olympia with Pliny's passionate interest in garden design. It is only at a far far later date that we find poets celebrating in fancy verse the calm and spaciousness of the municipal gardens at Alexandria.

Sappho, although she expresses regret that the shepherds should so wantonly trample the hyacinth under foot, is mainly interested in kitchen herbs. She mentions chervil, pulse, melilot and penny-royal. Sophocles writes of the petals of the narcissus and Callimachus of the 'sweet crocus'. But the habit of noticing the differences between flowers only came to the Greeks in much later times. Meleager, for instance, not only took delight in 'the lilies that haunt the hillside', the 'roses that are in love with love', but wrote two long poems comparing his friends to different flowers, poems that indicate not affection only, but also discrimination. Yet we have to wait to the dim distant Byzantine days of Rufinus, before we obtain any flower-picture in our modern sense:

> 'I send you, Rhodocleia, this garland of lovely flowers
> that I have woven with my own hands.'

> πέμπω σοι, ῾Ροδόκλεια, τόδε στέφος ἄνθεσι καλοῖς

It is rare in classical Greek to find sympathetic references to the smaller animals. As agriculturalists they were interested in livestock and bees; as racegoers and hunters they were expert on horses and sporting dogs; as people condemned to a sad monotony of diet they took a marked interest in the eels from Lake Copais. Every now and then they would write a pretty elegy on a Maltese poodle, and they were fond of tame quails and crickets, which they kept in grass cages and called, rather charmingly, the 'nightingale of the fields'. They did not, however, share our mass-veneration for pets; and to liken a man to a dog was an opprobrious act.

Their attitude to birds was, we must admit, conventional. They were fond of nightingales, since they represented, as Simonides and Sappho remarked, the coming of spring. But I cannot feel that such references to nightingales as occur in the opening section of the *Electra*, or even the famed Itys passage in the *Agamemnon*, display any very sympathetic interest in ornithology. Theocritus noticed and enjoyed the blackbird's song. Alcman certainly was fond of birds. 'I know', he writes, 'all the tunes that the birds sing.' But his mention of the 'sea-blue bird of March', ἀλιπόρφορος ἔαρος ὄρνις which Tennyson imitated with such felicity, does not in fact apply to the kingfisher, but to the halcyon, a bird of obscure identity and habits, who made her nest upon the waves of the sea. To this general ignorance of, or indifference to, the habits of birds there is of course one mighty exception. Aristophanes, in that he possessed, not wit only, but a vivid sense of humour, was also a sentimentalist. To him the tribes of birds were familiar and observed companions. It is not merely that in his great play he gives a detailed list of the birds of Attica; it is also that he had an instinctive love for their pathetic and inconsequent ways. Surely his ode to the nightingale can hold its own with any of our modern lyrics:

ὦ φίλη ὦ ζουθή
ὦ φίλτατον ὀρνέων
πάντων ξύννομε τῶν ἐμῶν
ὕμνων

Yet, apart from Aristophanes, the Greeks, I contend, were indifferent to the charm of little birds.

5

These illustrations and examples will, I trust, have sufficed to convince you that the Greek attitude to what we understand as the beauties of nature was wholly different from our own. This difference will become even more apparent when I pass from those effects of nature which either frightened or bored them to those by which they were deeply and seriously impressed.

One of the most constant and attractive of the many themes that inspire the Greek poets is their passion for the beauty and vigour of youth. Perhaps the only aspect of nature that affected them sentimentally was the advent of spring and the renewal of the youth and vigour of the soil. The Persephone myth was one that moved them with ever-recurring gladness and, as I have shown in so many of my illustrations, they responded most readily to those beauties of nature that were associated in their minds with the symbols of the coming spring. Unlike ourselves, the Greeks were not accustomed to identifying nature with the joys or miseries of mankind; but they did find some analogy between the freshness of early spring and the charms of human adolescence, by which they set much store. An outstanding example of this identification is the passage in the *Clouds*, where Aristophanes, in the

person of the Just Argument, bursts into anapaests
of truly lyrical fervour:

'Garlanded with the white reed, you will go down to
the Academy with some clean-minded friend of your own
age and run races underneath the olives. Smelling of
pollen and briony and ease of heart, rejoicing in the hour
of spring when the plane-tree whispers to the elm.'

ἦρος ἐν ὥρᾳ χαίρων ὁπόταν
πλάτανος πτελέᾳ ψιθυρίξῃ

The Greeks, as I have already indicated, were
extremely sensitive to cold. It was not only Homer
and Hesiod who loathed the north wind: Sophocles in
the *Antigone*, Euripides in the *Rhesus*, denounce the
chilly blasts from Thrace; each of them is sensitive
to 'the silver arrows of the snow'. The parching heat
of the Greek summer is also a constant theme of the
poets, leading them invariably to extol the delights of
shade and water, the charm of lush meadows beside
a stream:

'By the cool waterside [writes Sappho] the breeze stirs
the apple-branches and the quivering leaves shed sleep-
fulness.

'Oh to lie and dream, [writes Euripides in the *Hippolytus*]
in some grassy meadow in the poplar's shade.'

There can be no question but that for them the ideal
landscape was some sacred enclosure of trees and water,
such as Sophocles has described so affectionately in
Oedipus in Colonus. They did not care, as Wordsworth
cared, for nature in all her varying moods. They
desired only to find protection from the winds of
winter and shelter from the blazing summer sun. It is
noticeable that the epithet 'lovely' as applied to
external scenes is used only to refer to lawns and water.

Even Athens is not called 'lovely'; Pindar calls her 'divine' and 'glistening'; Bacchylides used the epithets 'happy' and 'splendour-loving'; and Plato in the *Protagoras* uses the fine phrase 'the sanctuary of wisdom'. But other places are called 'lovely'—Colophon by Mimnermus, Salamis by Solon; surely because they contained more glades than houses, meadows rather than temples.

It seems that night also, with the moon and stars, aroused in the Greek heart emotions that were partly religious, but also those of sensibility. There is a passage in Alcman in which he describes night in the mountains, when the beasts and birds are silent in sleep. Sappho has a famous passage about the moon and stars and in the *Phoenician Maidens* Euripides speaks of the moon's 'gold-encircled gleam', and notes the calm sombre motion with which she climbs the skies. The stars also have something more than a purely astronomical appeal. Plato in the *Republic* calls them 'these sparks that decorate the sky'. 'Hail black night,' says Electra, 'nurturer of the golden stars.' The watchman in the *Agamemnon* says how he has come to know 'the nightly assembly of the stars, those shining potentates that bring winter and summer unto men'. It is evident that the Greeks, like Pascal, were somewhat intimidated by the infinite silence of those vast spaces. Even the evening star, surely the gentlest of all, is spoken of with a sort of reverence. It is interesting to contrast the change in attitude marking the five hundred years that separate Sappho from Bion:

'Oh Hesperus [writes Sappho], you who bring back all that radiant dawn has scattered afar,—the sheep, the goat, the child home to its mother.

'Oh Hesperus [writes Bion], dear Hesperus, thou sacred jewel of the dark blue night.'

A lovely line, doubtless, but is it—or is it not—a trifle sentimental?

It was light and air that the Greeks loved most of all nature's manifestations. What beautiful and frequent words they had to express their sense of the shining or the glistening: λαμπρός and λιπαρός seem to me among the Greekest of all Greek words.

'Oh holy light,' exclaims Electra, 'oh wide surrounding air!' 'Oh unfoldings of ether,' writes Euripides, 'you shining spaces!' 'Sweet, sweet, is the sun-god's gleam,' he writes again. And in the *Rhesus* he shows a curiously un-Greek awareness of the effect of fading light when the tethered horses of Hector's Thracian chariot gleam at dusk, 'like the white wing of the river swan.'

Such instances and illustrations could be multiplied indefinitely. I have quoted enough to provide you with a representative sample. I have shown, I hope, that to the sea, scenery, mountains, forests, flowers and animals the Greeks were either indifferent or hostile. I have shown that their attitude towards the coming of spring, shade and water, air and sunshine and night and stars was one of reverence and pleasure. Can any general principles be deduced from such an analysis? I think they can.

6

One could dismiss the whole problem by stating that the Greeks were insensitive to the loveliness or variety of nature; and leave it at that. But this would surely be an incorrect conclusion. It would be absurd to contend that a people of such acute aesthetic perceptions could be indifferent to any form of loveliness. 'For surely', says Socrates in the *Republic*, 'the aim of culture is the passion for the beautiful.' Emotion even, was stated by Longinus to be one of the elements of the sublime. Nor would it be possible to say that the Greeks failed to notice the infinite variety of natural forms. The biological treatises of Aristotle and the astonishing range of subjects examined in the *Problemata* would disprove any such contention. It is safer, therefore, to assume that the Greeks approached nature with full awareness; but that their attitude was different from our own. Can we define that difference?

One might be tempted at this stage to employ the familiar contrast between 'Classical' and 'Romantic'; to identify the term 'Classical' with our own Augustan age, or with the French Age of Reason; and to ascribe the term 'Romantic' to the new forms of sensibility introduced by Thomson's *Seasons* in 1730 or by Young's *Night Thoughts* in 1742. Such analogies are helpful only in three negative respects.

It is true that the Greeks did not acquire the habit of our own Romantics of identifying man with nature. They did not—unless, as in the *Bacchae*, they were describing states of frenzy—attribute animate emotions to inanimate things. Keats' remark that he could 'peck with the sparrows in the gravel' would have seemed to them a meaningless and indeed comic observation. It is true also that they did not, as did our own Lake poets, find in nature some independent and mysterious power; they recognised her magic, but they attributed it, not to some vague concept called 'Nature', but to the gods of the sky or earth. It is true again that they did not find, or even seek for, some moral purpose or

influence in Nature such as inspired so much of Wordsworth's philosophy of life. 'One impulse', wrote
Wordsworth:

> *'One impulse from a vernal wood*
> *May teach you more of man,*
> *Of moral evil and of good,*
> *Than all the sages can.'*

'A sense sublime', he wrote again:

> *'A sense sublime*
> *Of something far more deeply interfused*
> *Whose dwelling is the light of setting suns,*
> *And the round ocean and the living air,*
> *And the blue sky, and in the mind of man.'*

'Such hues', wrote Coleridge, 'as veil the Almighty
Spirit.' These passages have for us an emotional
significance. To the Greeks they would have appeared,
not foolish merely, but also irreverent, presumptuous,
even impious.

Thus although the contrast between 'Classical' and
'Romantic', as employed in our sense of the terms,
does provide some information as to the manner in
which the Greeks did *not* feel or think, it is of little
assistance in elucidating the particular attitude towards
Nature that we recognise in their art and literature.
That attitude is to be explained rather by the importance that they attached to man and the importance that
they attached to the gods.

The Greek mind was objective rather than subjective; it expressed itself in the constructional rather than
in the representational, in shape rather than in colour,
in symmetry rather than in variety, in order more than in
confusion. 'The Greek', writes Sir Richard Living-

stone, 'shocks our sentimentality, for he has none of his own. He looks straight at life.' Thus, as Ruskin remarks in his admirable chapter on 'Classical Landscape', whereas the modern artist tries 'to express something which he, as a living creature, imagines in the lifeless object', the Greeks were 'content with expressing the unimaginary and actual qualities' of the things they observed. This natural lucidity induced them to be far more interested in the human foreground than in the natural background. Thus Plato insists that in any sculptural composition attention must be concentrated upon the human figures and the background merely adumbrated in shadowy form. To the Greeks of the great period the universe was to be interpreted by reason and not by sentiment. To them it is by the exercise of the human intellect, and not by the play of human senses, that we can hope to penetrate reality. From this aspect, Nature came to be subordinate for them to human nature; their measure of mankind was man.

'Nothing', wrote Sophocles in the *Antigone*, 'is more awe-inspiring than man.' The epithet that he used was that strange word δεινός. There is a passage in the *Phaedrus* that illustrates this attitude in very human terms. Socrates is walking with Phaedrus who leads him to the banks of the Ilissus where they can find water and shade. They paddle together in the stream:

' "By Hera!" remarks Socrates, "this is a delightful resting place. The plane-tree is wide and high, the willow delightful with its shade and moreover it is in full flower so that it scents the whole meadow. And how pretty is the spring as it bubbles up from underneath the plane-tree and the water is cool to my feet. . . . And all around us echoes the summer music of the crickets. But the most charming thing of all is this grass growing on the slope, thick enough to be perfect to lay the head down upon. . . . Truly, my dear Phaedrus, you have guided me most admirably." '

Phaedrus replies by expressing surprise that Socrates had never before visited the banks of the Ilissus. And then Socrates answers:—'Forgive me, my friend. You see, I am fond of learning (φιλομαθὴς γάρ εἰμι). Now meadows and trees won't teach me a thing. It is the people in town that instruct me.'

Does not this delightful dialogue remind us of the remark made by Dr. Johnson to Mrs. Thrale? 'A blade of grass', he thundered at her, 'is always a blade of grass. Men and women are *my* subjects of enquiry.'

This urban approach to Nature, this preference for the active exercise of human intelligence over the passive contemplation of natural beauty, is characteristic of any highly sophisticated age. Yet it is not possible to understand the Greek attitude without realising the effect upon their sensibilities of religious belief. For them, the loveliness of the external world was, if one may use so strained an expression, the personal property of the gods. A clue to their feelings on the subject (and I use the term 'feelings' advisedly) is provided, as Professor Hardie has pointed out, by the curious word ζάθεος. What did this epithet really imply? We translate it generally by our words 'sacred' or 'holy'. Yet in practice it is always applied to places regarded as specially favoured for their beauty by some god. Homer applies it to Tenedos, Euripides to Crete. It is used by Hesiod as an eulogy of the few winds that he did not detest. It applies to rivers and is frequently used as an epithet for caves. Why should a cave be regarded as ζάθεος? Surely because the word possessed some associations of mystery and awe, some religious attributes. To the Greeks the great manifestations of nature were associated with the Olympians. Poseidon ruled the sea; the mountains were the resort of divinities; the sun, the moon and the stars were the symbols of the immortals. It was an axiom of Greek religion that mortals should 'think mortal thoughts' and should never aspire to imitate the gods. To do so would be impious and might bring down on the offender the terrible penalties imposed on those guilty of hubris. Some of their reticence in regard to Nature can therefore be ascribed to the inhibitions induced by reverence.

Is it legitimate to push the argument further? We know that there existed in the Greek mind a distinction between the Olympian and the older chthonian gods, between the aetherial divinities and the non-aetherial, between the gods of heaven and the gods of earth. The Olympians represented sublimations of the divine in man: the earth divinities were in comparison sinister, mysterious, inimical. Is it too fantastic to suggest that the Greeks regarded the aetherial aspects of Nature—air and sunlight, springtime and cool meadows; the moon and the stars—as having Olympian attributes; and that the more earthly aspects, as being suggestive of the chthonian deities, were for them subjects of reticence and alarm?

Some clue to the importance attached to light and air is afforded by the, to us, baffling inability of the Greeks to differentiate between colours. How came it that a race so endowed with aesthetic perception should have possessed so few words to describe colour and have used these few words carelessly and without discrimination? The explanation surely is, not that the Greeks were afflicted with universal colour blindness, but that they were interested in form rather than in colour, in texture rather than in pigmentation; and that they measured colour, not in shades as we do, but in different qualities of light.

You will recall that among the Aristotelian note-books collected by the Peripatetic School there is an essay on colours, which confirms this suggestion. In commenting upon the many variations of what the Greeks called purple, the author adds that colours can be distinguished according as they are bright or dark. 'A bright colour', he says, 'is nothing but the continuity and intensity of light.' Even the Romans drew a distinction between colours seen in light and colours seen in shade. Thus they had two words for black—*niger* and *ater*—and two words for white—*candidus* and *albus*—applying the former two when they meant glistening black or white, and the latter two when they meant black or white that were darkened by shade.

But I have said enough to indicate the immense importance attached by the ancients to illumination. In conclusion, I leave it to those who have made a profound study of Greek religion to decide whether the hypothesis is tenable that the Greeks identified the aetherial aspects of Nature with joy and pleasure, and the Earth aspects with anxiety and distress.

The idea is not one that I should willingly surrender. Since it enables me to approach Greek nature poetry as something associated with the most entrancing of all Greek qualities, with the qualities of lucidity, gaiety and light.